AMAZING ANIMALS
OF THE WORLD 2

Volume 9

Snakefly — Toad, Surinam

GROLIER

First published 2005 by Grolier, an imprint of Scholastic Library Publishing

For information address the publisher: Grolier, Scholastic Library Publishing
90 Old Sherman Turnpike
Danbury, CT 06816

Set ISBN: 0-7172-6112-3; Volume ISBN: 0-7172-6121-2

Printed and bound in the U.S.A.

Library of Congress Cataloging-in-Publications Data:
Amazing animals of the world 2.
p.cm.
Includes indexes.
Contents: v. 1. Adder—Buffalo, Water -- v. 2. Bunting, Corn—Cricket, Bush -- v. 3. Cricket, European Mole—Frog, Agile -- v. 4. Frog, Burrowing Tree—Guenon, Moustached -- v. 5. Gull, Great Black-backed—Loach, Stone -- v. 6. Locust, Migratory—Newt, Crested -- v. 7. Nuthatch, Eurasian—Razor, Pod -- v. 8. Reedbuck, Mountain—Snake, Tentacled -- v. 9. Snakefly—Toad, Surinam -- v. 10. Tortoise, Gopher—Zebu.
ISBN 0-7172-6112-3 (set : alk. paper) -- ISBN 0-7172-6113-1 (v. 1 : alk. paper) -- ISBN 0-7172-6114-X (v. 2 : alk. paper) -- ISBN 0-7172-6115-8 (v. 3 : alk. paper) -- ISBN 0-7172-6116-6 (v. 4 : alk. paper) -- ISBN 0-7172-6117-4 (v. 5 : alk. paper) -- ISBN 0-7172-6118-2 (v. 6 : alk. paper) -- ISBN 0-7172-6119-0 (v. 7 : alk. paper) -- ISBN 0-7172-6120-4 (v. 8 : alk. paper) -- ISBN 0-7172-6121-2 (v. 9 : alk. paper) -- ISBN 0-7172-6122-0 (v. 10 : alk.paper)
1. Animals--Juvenile literature. I. Title: Amazing animals of the world two. II. Grolier (Firm)
QL49.A455 2005
590--dc22
                                                                                    2005040351

About This Set

Amazing Animals of the World 2 brings you pictures of 400 fascinating creatures and important information about how and where they live.

Each page shows just one species—individual type—of animal. They all fall into seven main categories or groups of animals (classes and phylums scientifically) that appear on each page as an icon or picture—amphibians, arthropods, birds, fish, mammals, other invertebrates, and reptiles. Short explanations of what these group names mean, and other terms used commonly in the set, appear on page 4 in the Glossary.

Scientists use all kinds of groupings to help them sort out the thousands of types of animals that exist today and once wandered here (extinct species). Kingdoms, classes, phylums, genus, and species are among the key words here that are also explained in the Glossary (page 4).

Where animals live is important to know as well. Each of the species in this set lives in a particular place in the world, which you can see outlined on the map on each page. And in those locales the animals tend to favor a particular habitat—an environment the animal finds suitable for life, with food, shelter, and safety from predators that might eat it. There they also find ways to coexist with other animals in the area that might eat somewhat different food, use different homes, and so on. Each of the main habitats is named on the page and given an icon/picture to help you envision it. The habitat names are further defined in the Glossary on page 4.

As well as being part of groups like species, animals fall into other categories that help us understand their lives or behavior. You will find these categories in the Glossary on page 4, where you will learn about carnivores, herbivores, and other types of animals.

And there is more information you might want about an animal—its size, diet, where it lives, and how it carries on its species—the way it creates its young. All these facts and more appear in the data boxes at the top of each page.

Finally, you should know that the set is arranged alphabetically by the most common name of the species. That puts most beetles, say, together in a group so you can compare them easily.

But some animals' names are not so common, and they don't appear near others like them. For instance, the chamois is a kind of goat or antelope. To find animals that are similar—or to locate any species—look in the index at the end of each book in the set (pages 45-48). It lists all animals by their various names (you will find the giant South American river turtle under turtle, giant South American river, and also under its other name—arrau). And you will find all birds, fish, and so on gathered under their broader groupings.

Similarly, smaller like groups appear in the set index as well—butterflies include swallowtails and blues, for example.

Table of Contents
Volume 9

Glossary...4

Snakefly...5

Snipefish, Longspine..6

Sole, European..7

Solenodon, Haitian...8

Spadefish...9

Spadefoot, European..10

Sparrow, American Tree...11

Sparrow, Hedge...12

Sparrow, Java..13

Spider, Goldenrod...14

Sponge, Fire..15

Sponge, Purple Column (Giant Tube Sponge)................................16

Sponge, Stinker..17

Sponge, Vase...18

Springbok...19

Squirrel, Golden-mantled Ground..20

Star, Slime...21

Starling, Superb..22

Stentor, Blue..23

Stonechat...24

Stork, White...25

Sungazer..26

Surgeonfish, Powder-blue..27

Suricate (Meerkat)..28

Swallowtail, Common European...29

Swan, Whooper..30

Swordtail..31

Tahr, Himalayan..32

Tanager, Scarlet..33

Tapeworm, Cat...34

Tarsier, Western...35

Tenrec, Lesser Hedgehog...36

Tern, Whiskered...37

Tetra, Bleeding-heart..38

Tetra, Glowlight...39

Thrush, Mistle..40

Thrush, Rock..41

Toad, Eurasian Common..42

Toad, Green..43

Toad, Surinam..44

Set Index..45

Glossary

Amphibians—species usually born from eggs in water or wet places, which change (metamorphose) into a land animal. Frogs and salamanders are typical. They breathe through their skin mainly and have no scales.

Arctic and Antarctic—icy, cold, dry areas at the ends of the globe that lack trees but see small plants grown in thawed areas (tundra). Penguins and seals are common inhabitants.

Arthropods—animals with segmented bodies, hard outer skin, and jointed legs, such as spiders and crabs.

Birds—born from eggs, these creatures have wings and often can fly. Eagles, pigeons, and penguins are all birds, though penguins can't fly through the air.

Carnivores—they are animals that eat other animals. Many species do eat each other sometimes, and a few eat dead animals. Lions kill their prey and eat it, while vultures clean up dead bodies of animals.

Cities, Towns, and Farms—places where people live and have built or used the land and share it with many species. Sometimes these animals live in human homes or just nearby.

Class—part or division of a phylum.

Deserts—dry, often warm areas where animals often are more active on cooler nights or near water sources. Owls, scorpions, and jack rabbits are common in American deserts.

Endangered—some animals in this set are marked as endangered because it is possible they will become extinct soon.

Extinct—these species have died out altogether for whatever reason.

Family—part of an order.

Fish—water animals (aquatic) that typically are born from eggs and breathe through gills. Trout and eels are fish, though whales and dolphins are not (they are mammals).

Forests and Mountains—places where evergreen (coniferous) and leaf-shedding (deciduous) trees are common, or that rise in elevation to make cool, separate habitats. **Rainforests are different (see below).**

Fresh Water—lakes, rivers, and the like carry fresh water (unlike Oceans and Shores, where the water is salty). Fish and birds abound, as do insects, frogs, and mammals.

Genus—part of a family.

Grasslands—habitats with few trees and light rainfall. Grasslands often lie between forests and deserts, and they are home to birds, coyotes, antelope, and snakes, as well as many other kinds of animals.

Herbivores—these animals eat mainly plants. Typical are hoofed animals (ungulates) that are common on grasslands, such as antelope or deer. Domestic (nonwild) ones are cows and horses.

Hibernators—species that live in harsh areas with very cold winters slow down their functions then and sort of sleep through the hard times.

Kingdom—the largest division of species. Commonly there are understood to be five kingdoms: animals, plants, fungi, protists, and monerans.

Mammals—these creatures usually bear live young and feed them on milk from the mother. A few lay eggs (monotremes like the platypus) or nurse young in a pouch (marsupials like opossums and kangaroos).

Migrators—some species spend different seasons in different places, moving to where more food, warmth, or safety can be found. Birds often do this, sometimes over long distances, but others types of animals also move seasonally, including fish and mammals.

Oceans and Shores—seawater is salty, often deep, and huge. In it live many fish, invertebrates, and even some mammals, such as whales. On the shore birds and other creatures often gather.

Order—part of a class.

Other Invertebrates—animals that lack backbones or internal skeletons. Many, such as insects and shrimp, have hard outer coverings. Clams and worms are also invertebrates.

Phylum—part of a kingdom.

Rainforests—here huge trees grow among many other plants helped by the warm, wet environment. Thousands of species of animals also live in these rich habitats.

Reptiles—these species have scales, lungs to breathe, and lay eggs or give birth to live young. Dinosaurs are thought to have been reptiles, while today the class includes turtles, snakes, lizards, and crocodiles.

Scientific name—the genus and species name of a creature in Latin. For instance, Canis lupus is the wolf. Scientific names avoid the confusion possible with common names in any one language or across languages.

Species—a group of the same type of living thing. Part of an order.

Subspecies—a variant but quite similar part of a species.

Territorial—many animals mark out and defend a patch of ground as their home area. Birds and mammals may call quite small or quite large spots their territories.

Vertebrates—animals with backbones and skeletons under their skins

Snakefly
Raphidia notata

Length: about 1 inch
Wingspan: about 1 inch
Diet: soft-bodied insects
Method of Reproduction: egg layer

Home: North America, Eurasia, and northern Africa
Order: Snakeflies
Family: Common snakeflies

 Forests and Mountains

 Arthropods

© KIM TAYLOR / BRUCE COLEMAN INC.

The snakefly is named for its long, snakelike neck. The female is easily recognized by her long, stingerlike "ovipositor." Although it looks like a dangerous stinger, an ovipositor is used only to lay eggs. Female snakeflies lay their eggs deep in the crevices of trees that are infested with beetle larvae. Beetle larvae are serious pests that damage trees. The beneficial snakefly inserts her eggs on or near the beetles. The beetles are then eaten by the young snakeflies when they hatch.

Snakeflies prefer to live on oak trees, although they can also be found in pine woods. Both the adults and their young eat destructive insects. Researchers have tried, without success, to breed snakeflies for use in controlling insect pests in problem areas. However, the snakefly appears to be too rare and delicate to be raised in large numbers. Its cousin, the lacewing, is better suited for this job of "biocontrol."

When they are ready to transform into adults, young snakeflies crawl down tree trunks and dig small chambers in the ground. These immature snakeflies may spend as long as two years under the ground. Every other spring, they emerge in large numbers as adults. This emergence can usually be seen at a very early morning hour. The new adults cannot immediately fly. First they must slowly stretch and dry their wings in the morning sun.

Longspine Snipefish
Macrorhamphosus scolopax

Length: up to 8 inches
Diet: plankton and worms and other invertebrates
Method of Reproduction: egg layer

Home: temperate seas worldwide
Order: Sticklebacks and their relatives
Family: Snipefishes

 Oceans and Shores

 Fish

© TAVERNIER / NAUSICAA / PETER ARNOLD, INC.

The longspine snipefish is a very flat fish that resembles a barely filled envelope. This particular species is named for the long, thick spine that grows from its dorsal fin (located along its back). Like all snipefish, this species has a long, tubular snout that ends in a small, toothless mouth. The snipefish feeds by vacuuming up tiny plankton animals floating in the water and small worms buried in the soil. The longspine snipefish, in turn, is eaten by tuna, marlin, and other ocean predators.

This small ocean fish is a weak swimmer. It usually rides from place to place on the ocean currents. When young, snipefish tend to drift near the surface. Older individuals stay closer to the bottom of the ocean.

Longspine snipefish are not common. However, the young fish are occasionally seen in enormous schools in water that is between 200 and 650 feet deep. Fishermen accidentally catch adult longspines while trawling the ocean bottom in places such as the Georges Bank, near Cape Cod, Massachusetts.

The snipefish's flat body has several bony plates on each side. The plates on its chest area form a sharp keel that cuts through the water like the front of a narrow canoe. Most longspine snipefish are reddish or golden on the upper half of their body and silvery white below. Very young snipefish are silver with a bluish-black back.

6

European Sole
Solea solea

Length: 1 to 1½ feet
Weight: 5 to 10 pounds
Diet: mollusks and worms
Method of Reproduction: egg layer

Home: Atlantic Ocean, North Sea, English Channel, Baltic Sea, and Mediterranean Sea
Order: Flatfishes
Family: Soles

  Oceans and Shores

Fish

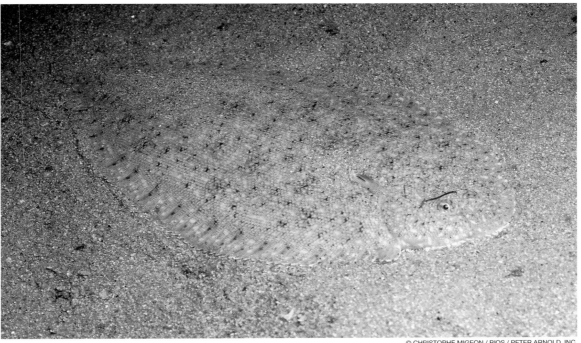

© CHRISTOPHE MIGEON / BIOS / PETER ARNOLD, INC.

Today many kind sole are sold as"fillets" in grocery stores and on restaurant menus. But the European sole was the first, and, to some people, it remains the tastiest. European sole is still popular in fish markets throughout Europe and is also flown fresh to North American markets. The European sole's appearance varies within its species. Experts can tell where a European sole was caught by the color of its skin and meat.

Like other soles, the European species lives at the bottom of the sea. There it hunts through the night, searching the sand for small sea animals. A nighttime hunter, the sole cannot rely on its eyesight to find its prey. But nature has equipped the fish with an exceptional sense of smell. Scientists have found special tubelike structures on the underside of the sole's flat head. These organs are thought to enhance the sole's sense of smell.

The European sole is a particularly lopsided fish. By its picture, you can see that both of the sole's eyes are on top of its pancake-shaped body. But its mouth is nowhere to be seen. Soles, like other flatfish, are born looking like "normal" fish—with an eye on each side of the body and a mouth at the front. But by the time most flatfish grow to the size of a penny, both eyes and nostrils have moved to one side. The sole looks even more twisted than most flatfish because its mouth travels to the opposite side of its head from its eyes and nose.

Haitian Solenodon
Solenodon paradoxus

Length of the Body: 11 to 13 inches

Length of the Tail: 7 to 10 inches

Diet: mainly insects and other invertebrates

Number of Young: 1 to 3

Home: Haiti and the Dominican Republic

Weight: 1⅓ to 2¼ pounds

Order: Insectivores

Family: Solenodons

 Rainforests

 Mammals

© N. SMYTHE / PHOTO RESEARCHERS

Endangered Animals

The Haitian solenodon, with its long snout, large ears, and tiny eyes, resembles an oversized shrew. Yet it is only distantly related to shrews and other insectivores. In fact, its one living relative is the Cuban solenodon. Millions of years ago, solenodons may have been much more common. Fossil remains suggest that they once lived in North America. Today the two species are on the brink of extinction. They have survived this long, scientists say, because they have no natural competitors on their island homes. However, dogs, cats, mongooses, and other animals introduced to the islands have killed a great many of these creatures. Also, humans have destroyed much of the animals' habitat.

The Haitian solenodon hunts at night, moving slowly through the underbrush of rainforests and wet, subtropical areas. Its favorite prey includes millipedes, ground beetles, and earthworms. It also opens snails and bitter oranges to get at the tasty food inside. In the morning, solenodons retreat to their dens, where they sleep cuddled together with several family members. Up to eight individuals may share a cave, rock crevice, or hollow log.

Solenodons are among the few mammals with a venomous bite. Their toxic saliva is injected through grooved teeth at the front of the mouth. The saliva is deadly to small prey, but merely painful to humans.

8

Spadefish
Platax pinnatus

Length: up to 18 inches
Diet: small invertebrates
Method of Reproduction: egg layer

Home: tropical waters of the Indian and Pacific oceans
Order: Perchlike fishes
Family: Spadefishes

 Oceans and Shores

 Fish

© SECRET SEA VISIONS / PETER ARNOLD, INC.

The spectacularly beautiful spadefish has a very long body that is narrow from side to side. It has two huge fins—one on the top (dorsal) surface of the body and one on the lower (ventral) surface. These large, winglike fins give rise to two other common names for the fish: "long-finned batfish" and "seabat."

Spadefish live in shallow tropical waters close to shore. They particularly like mangrove swamps, where they swim among the underwater roots of the mangrove trees. Sometimes spadefish float on their side and allow themselves to be rolled about by the slowly moving water. In this position, they look like dead leaves. Imitating dead leaves is good protection against predators.

Disappearing quickly among the tangle of tree roots is another form of protection.

Very young spadefish look somewhat like mollusks called nudibranchs. This resemblance protects the young spadefish because nudibranchs are not tasty, and predators avoid them. Young spadefish are yellow or orange, with dark vertical stripes. As the fish age, the stripes fade.

Some people raise spadefish in aquariums. Young specimens grow very rapidly and quickly become too big for home aquariums. They also aren't suited for home aquariums because they are very aggressive toward other fish. The best place to view these beautiful fish is in a public aquarium.

European Spadefoot
Pelobates fuscus

Length: 2 to 3 inches
Weight: 5 ounces
Diet: worms, algae, plants, and small pond organisms
Number of Eggs: 750

Home: western Asia and Central Europe
Order: Frogs, toads, and tree toads
Family: Spadefoot toads

 Fresh Water

Amphibians

© BERNDT FISCHER / BIOS / PETER ARNOLD, INC.

The European spadefoot gets its name from the hard little shovel-shaped horns on the inside of its feet. It uses these sharp-edged spades to burrow into the sand with amazing speed. Like other spade-footed toads, the European spadefoot spends its entire day in a sandy hole. There it can stay moist and keep safe from owls and other predators. The European spadefoot is very reclusive—in fact, it is rarely seen. Despite its infrequent appearances, however, the European variety is the most common of all spadefoots.

The spadefoot toad has been called the "gnome of the night," because only after sunset does it pop out of its hole to search for food or to mate. The European spadefoot's breeding season is quite long, from April to June. During this time the toads congregate in ponds and large puddles.

The male European spadefoot has a special underwater mating call. Although its call is little more than a loud buzzing sound, it is usually enough to coax a female into view. If the female rubs up against the male, he will grasp her around the waist and climb on her back. The female toad may try to scrape off her suitor by sliding under a nearby rock. But male spadefoots are persistent. As the female tries to shake him loose, the male will slide his arms up and down her body to maintain a firm grip. Eventually the female will release her eggs—about a thousand, all tucked inside a short, thick rope of jelly.

American Tree Sparrow
Spizella arborea

Length: 5½ to 6½ inches
Wingspan: 8½ to 9¾ inches
Weight: about ¾ ounce
Diet: mainly seeds
Number of Eggs: 3 to 6

Home: United States and Canada
Order: Perching birds
Family: Finches

 Grasslands

 Birds

☐ Summer
☐ Winter

Despite its name, the American tree sparrow is hardly a tree dweller. In fact, this bird lives mainly in fields, marshes, and tundra. Alaska and Canada, the sparrow's summer home, are also its nesting grounds. In fall the bird migrates south. It may travel as much as 3,000 miles—the distance between New York and California—between its summer and winter homes!

The American tree sparrow feeds on the ground. Its strong, cone-shaped bill is perfect for cracking open seeds. The sparrow eats huge amounts of seeds, including those of many weeds. It also is a common visitor to bird feeders and supplements its diet with insects or spiders.

During much of the year, American tree sparrows live in flocks usually containing 30 to 40 birds. After the spring migration north, the birds go their separate ways. Each male stakes out his own territory before courting and mating with a female.

The typical sparrow nest is made on or near the ground, in clumps of grass, mounds of moss, or low shrubs or trees. The female builds the nest, using plant matter such as grass and moss, and lines the nest with bird feathers and bits of animal fur. The eggs are incubated for about 12 days before they hatch. Unlike many birds, baby sparrows seem to rush out of the nest—often departing when they're only 10 days old!

Hedge Sparrow
Prunella modularis

Length: up to 6 inches
Diet: insects, grubs, and seeds
Number of Eggs: 3 to 6

Home: Europe and Asia
Order: Perching birds
Family: Accentors

 Forests and Mountains

 Birds

© ROBERT MAIER / ANIMALS ANIMALS / EARTH SCENES

The hedge sparrow, known in England as the dunnock, is a drab brown bird with a weak but pleasant song. It sings almost all year round, with a high piping "tseep" and a short trilling jingle. Unfortunately, its cheery little song is usually drowned out by the racket of noisier birds such as the starling.

True to its name, this bird prefers to nest in hedges and bushes. In spring, hedge sparrows weave neat, cup-shaped nests out of twigs, grasses, and stringy rootlets. The female incubates the eggs, and her mate helps feed the young when they hatch. If the summer is long and pleasant, hedge sparrows often raise a second brood of chicks, after the first batch has left the nest.

The hedge sparrow spends much of its time on the ground, usually alone, searching for insects and their larvae. It hunts among fallen leaves, usually under the cover of low bushes and trees. There it walks with a slow, shuffling gait, twitching its wings to stir up dust and insects.

The name "sparrow" has come to include any small, roundish bird with drab, streaked feathers. The tiny brown hedge sparrow certainly fits this description. But true sparrows have stout, short beaks, built for cracking seeds. In contrast, the hedge sparrow has a delicate, narrow bill, more suited for picking up insects and larvae. It eats seeds only when it must, usually in winter, when insects are scarce.

Java Sparrow
Padda oryzivora

Length: up to 6 inches
Weight: up to 1 ounce
Diet: mainly rice and other seeds
Number of Eggs: up to 8

Home: native to Java and Bali; introduced to other tropical islands
Order: Perching birds
Family: Weaverfinches

 Cities, Towns, and Farms

 Birds

© HANS REINHARD / BRUCE COLEMAN INC.

With its black, white, and brown feathers, the Java sparrow is an exception in a family of colorful tropical birds—the weaverfinches. Among its close cousins are the blue-faced parrotfinch and the red-cheeked cordon-bleu. Yet the Java sparrow is anything but dull. It is handsomely patterned and is a much-loved and lively cage bird.

Originally this species lived only on the islands of Java and Bali in the South Pacific. Over the years, sailors and other travelers transported it to several other tropical islands. Several of these introductions occurred when pet Java sparrows escaped from their cages. As a result, these birds now live in the wild on the islands of the Seychelles and Zanzibar in the Indian Ocean, on St. Helena in the Atlantic, and throughout the Hawaiian Islands.

Java sparrows are very social birds that fly in large, chattering flocks. Seed eaters by nature, they glean fallen seeds off the ground and climb up stalks and tree limbs to pluck fresh grain. Farmers consider the sparrows pests because the birds have acquired a taste for rice. A large flock can easily destroy a farmer's entire crop.

Java sparrows weave dome-shaped nests between the forked branches of a tree or under the eaves of buildings. Their eggs hatch about two weeks after they are laid. The parents feed their chicks mashed insects.

Goldenrod Spider
Misumena vatia

Length: ⅓ to ½ inch (female);
⅛ to ⅙ inch (male)
Diet: flying insects
Method of Reproduction: egg
layer

Home: North America and
Europe
Order: Spiders
Family: Crab spiders

Cities, Towns,
and Farms

Arthropods

© KAREN TWEEDY-HOLMES / CORBIS

The goldenrod spider spins silk, but it does not build a web as most spiders do. Instead, goldenrod spiders sit patiently on the blooms of goldenrod, Queen Anne's lace, and several other plants. There they wait for insects to visit the flowers, looking for pollen and nectar. The goldenrod spider sits with its front legs outstretched, ready to snatch an insect the moment it arrives. As soon as this waiting predator has grabbed its prey, the spider bites. The goldenrod spider will hold tight with its clenched jaws until the insect has stopped struggling. Then the spider chews its meal.

The goldenrod spider is a very successful hunter because its victims seldom see the creature until it is too late. Why? The goldenrod spider can alter its color to match certain flowers. But this spider is no fast-change artist. It takes the goldenrod spider 10 days to completely change color. This ability to camouflage itself also helps the goldenrod spider avoid being eaten by birds.

Baby goldenrod spiders hatch in spring and feed all summer, moving from one plant to another during the season. In August, female spiders lay their eggs. They place the eggs in silken sacs on leaves. Then they fold the leaf over the eggs and use more silk to seal the leaf into a little package. This protects the eggs until they hatch the following spring.

Fire Sponge
Tedania ignis

Width: about 1 foot
Height: about 1 foot
Diet: plankton and dissolved organic matter
Methods of Reproduction: spores and budding

Home: Caribbean Sea and coastal Atlantic waters from Florida to Mexico
Order: Cornacuspongid sponges
Family: Tedaniid sponges

 Oceans and Shores

Other Invertebrates

© E.R. DEGGINGER / COLOR-PIC INC.

This animal's name describes its color and its dangerous sting. The bright red or red-orange warns "Don't touch!" in the strongest of terms. Toxic chemicals in the fire sponge can cause great pain and blistering to unprotected skin. The sponge's color resembles that of another dangerous species: the "do-not-touch-me" sponge. Because both can cause injury, snorkelers are wise to avoid any red sponges in the waters around Florida, the Bahamas, and the Caribbean.

The fire sponge has good reason to be unfriendly—its soft, squishy body is easily torn and damaged. Helping it survive, its toxic chemicals discourage the slightest

touch by fish, crabs, or humans. Fire sponges grow in bays, lagoons, and other shallow seaways. They seldom survive in water deeper than about 50 feet. Nor does the sponge venture above the low-tide line; it dries out quickly when exposed to air.

When young, the sponge anchors its body to a rock or other solid object. It can then grow to a massive size. Compared with other sponges, this species has a smoother surface, with just a few large pores. Like most sponges, it reproduces by sending out spores, which then mature into adult sponges. An adult sponge can also replicate by "budding," in which cells on the surface begin growth as tiny new sponges.

Purple Column (Giant Tube) Sponge
Aplysina lacunosa

Width: 1 to 1½ inches
Length: up to 2 feet
Methods of Reproduction:
  egg laying and cloning

Diet: plankton
Home: Caribbean Sea
Order: Basket sponges
Family: Aplysinid sponges

Oceans and Shores

Other Invertebrates

© CHARLES V. ANGELO / PHOTO RESEARCHERS

The purple column, or giant tube, sponge spends its life attached to coral reefs, often in deep water. The sponge's body is a large, hollow cylinder with thick walls. Many of these sponges are dark blue or a pinkish lavender. Others are yellow or reddish brown. Two to four purple column sponges can live attached together at a common base; others live singly.

As a column sponge grows, its body is shaped by its environment. A sponge growing in calm water, for example, may be tall and straight. But if a strong ocean current pulls and pushes at the sponge, it may grow to be wide and short. Like most sponges, this species can survive a lot of damage. If it is broken into pieces, most of the pieces can grow into new, complete sponges.

Like most sponges, this species takes in food through many pores, or small holes, in its body. Inside the pores are cells with tiny hairs that beat the water. This motion draws in floating plankton and other tiny foodstuffs.

A purple column sponge can multiply by generating small buds. Budding always produces individuals that are identical to their parent. The sponge can also reproduce sexually. It does so by sending a large cloud of sperm into the water. The sperm floats into other column sponges and fertilizes the eggs inside their bodies.

Stinker Sponge
Ircinia fasciculata

Height: 12 inches
Width: 8 inches
Diet: microscopic organisms
Method of Reproduction:
  sexually and asexually

Home: Caribbean Sea and
  Gulf of Mexico
Order: Heterocoela
Family: Leuconidae

 Oceans and Shores

 Other Invertebrates

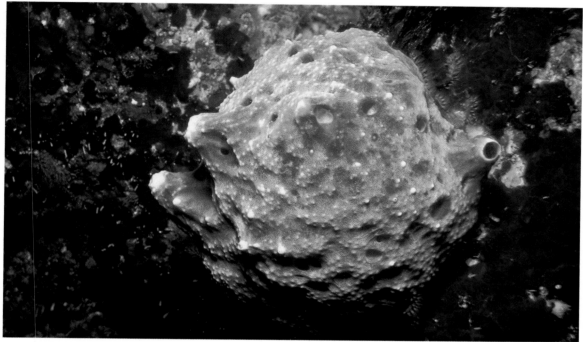

© DINO SIMEONIDIS / PETER ARNOLD, INC.

Most sponges give off an unpleasant smell. But the stinker sponge really stinks! Scientists believe that the awful odor protects the sponge from being eaten by hungry predators. Stinker sponges live in warm, shallow seas, almost always at depths of less than 50 feet. The stinker sponge has no eyes, no ears, and no feelers. It also lacks a heart, brain, stomach, and muscles. Yet it is classified as an animal. The main thing that makes the stinker sponge an animal is the way it gets food. It does not make its own food, as plants do. Instead, it captures tiny organisms from its surroundings.

The stinker sponge is built like a hollow bag, with an opening at the upper end. The bottom end is attached to a rock or other solid surface. A skeleton gives the stinker its shape. Water carrying food enters the sponge through tiny holes in the sides. The water passes through the sponge and then flows out through the opening at the top. Food is caught on the surfaces of cells on the inside of the sponge.

The most common method of reproduction in the stinker sponge is budding. A tiny sponge grows from the side of the parent. This bud may separate and begin life as a new individual. The bud sometimes remains attached to the parent, together with other buds. Stinker sponges are often found in such clusters.

Vase Sponge
Ircinia campana

Length: 2 feet
Diameter: 2 feet
Weight: 1 pound
Diet: bacterial plankton
Number of Eggs: 2,000 to 4,000

Home: Caribbean Sea from the Bahamas to Brazil
Order: Concave-shaped sponges
Family: Vase sponges

 Oceans and Shores

 Other Invertebrates

© FRED BAVENDAM / PETER ARNOLD, INC.

This particular species of vase sponge sometimes carries a less complimentary name: the stinking vase sponge. If you want to know why, just pull one out of the water! Though it smells foul, the vase sponge looks beautiful in its natural environment. In order to maintain its elegant, vaselike shape, the sponge must sit in water that flows slowly in only one direction. A fast-moving current or a crosscurrent will compress the vase sponge into the shape of a fan. If, on the other hand, the sponge gets stuck in water that doesn't move at all, it will smother from the dirt and debris that settles into its large, vaselike opening.

If you were to touch this creature's "vase," it would feel hard and coarse. This is the animal's external skeleton. Hidden within it is the sponge's soft body.

Like many sponges, the vase sponge provides a home for small crabs and shrimp who like to live in the large holes in the sponge's skeleton. These guests sometimes nibble away at their host. But the sponge quickly replaces the lost tissue, so little damage is done. One live-in guest actually benefits the vase sponge. The sponge harbors a tiny alga in its flesh. The alga passes nutrients into the sponge's cells and, at the same time, carries out the sponge's waste products. The arrangement works well for both creatures because the sponge's garbage is the alga's food.

Springbok
Antidorcas marsupialis

Length of the Body: 4 to 5 feet
Length of the Tail: 8 to 12 inches
Weight: 44 to 99 pounds
Diet: grasses, herbs, leaves, and roots

Number of Young: 1
Home: southern Africa
Order: Even-toed hoofed mammals
Family: Bovines
Subfamily: Antelopes

 Grasslands

 Mammals

© MARTIN HARVEY / GALLO IMAGES / CORBIS

A springbok's idea of fun is to bounce straight up in the air. South Africans call this odd hopping behavior "pronking." Just before a springbok "pronks," it lowers its head and arches its back like a bucking bronco. Then it springs off the ground, kicking with all four legs. As soon as the springbok lands, it rockets off the ground again, often to amazing heights.

Both male and female springboks have elegant ringed horns, although the female's are shorter and lighter. Another special trait is a crest of long, bristly white hairs on the top of the springbok's rump. When a springbok is frightened, these rump hairs stand straight up.

Like many antelope, the springbok lives in large herds. But rather than forming harems, where one male rules many females, springboks live in mixed groups for most of the year. In spring the adult males become restless and leave the herd. Then each male tries to tempt a female to follow him. If he's successful, he will lead her to a secluded hideaway where they can mate.

Springboks travel long distances in their search for food. In years past, huge migrating herds did considerable damage to the country through which they passed. But today hunting and the destruction of the springbok's grassy home have greatly reduced the animal's numbers.

Golden-mantled Ground Squirrel
Spermophilus lateralis

Length of the Body: 9 to 12 inches
Length of the Tail: 2½ to 4½ inches
Weight: 6 to 10 ounces
Diet: seeds, nuts, and fruits

Number of Young: 4 to 6
Home: western Canada and the United States
Order: Rodents
Family: Squirrels

  Forests and Mountains

Mammals

© D. ROBERT & LORRI FRANZ / CORBIS

The golden-mantled ground squirrel, also called the "copperhead," is named for the shiny red fur on its head and shoulders. This squirrel very much resembles a chipmunk and is only a little larger. But look closely, and you will see that, unlike chipmunks, ground squirrels have no stripes on their face. They can be recognized by the rings of white fur around their eyes.

Golden-mantled ground squirrels are most abundant on the slopes of the Rocky Mountains and in forests to the west. They are often seen rolling in the dust, which they use to clean their fur coats. After dust bathing, the ground squirrel carefully combs its fur with its teeth and claws. Golden-mantled ground squirrels sit upright as they preen—so they can scan for approaching enemies.

While other squirrel species tend to scold and chatter, golden-mantled squirrels keep unusually silent. They chirp and squeal only when frightened. Sometimes they growl quietly when fighting with one another.

The golden-mantled ground squirrel gives birth in early summer and spends the rest of the season fattening up for winter. In late October, as it prepares to hibernate, the squirrel stuffs its cheek pouches full with fruits, nuts, and seeds. It then curls up inside its underground burrow and goes to sleep for five or six months. Occasionally it will waken for a few hours to snack on the food stashed away in its cheeks.

Slime Star
Pteraster tesselatus

Length: up to 4¾ inches
Number of Arms: 5
Diet: sponges and other invertebrates
Method of Reproduction: live-bearer

Home: Bering Sea and Pacific coasts of North America and Asia
Order: Spinulosid starfishes
Family: Pterasterid starfishes

 Oceans and Shores

 Other Invertebrates

© FRED BAVENDAM / PETER ARNOLD, INC.

Dare to disturb a slime star, and you will quickly learn how it got its name. In just a minute or two, this starfish can coat itself—and everything around it—with a layer of ooze. This goop comes in handy when the slime star is attacked. Few creatures can get a good grip on the slippery mess. And those that do will find the slime filled with poisonous chemicals. The slime star is unique among starfish for another reason as well. It grows an inflatable membrane, or chamber, over the top of its body. The slime star breathes by pulling water in and out of this pouch.

Females deposit their eggs directly into their breathing chambers. This keeps the eggs safe from predators and ensures that the eggs receive a constant supply of fresh water. When they hatch, the young slime stars remain inside the chamber for a time, then slip out and drift away.

The slime star has a huge appetite for sea sponges and anemones. Sometimes the slime star eats its prey whole. The creature wraps its arms around its live meal and presses the animal into its round mouth. This mouth is located like a belly button on the middle of the slime star's underbelly. The slime star can also eat sponges and anemones much larger than itself. To do so, it pushes part of its stomach out through its mouth and directly onto the food.

Superb Starling
Spreo superbus

Length: about 7 inches
Diet: insects and berries
Number of Eggs: usually 4

Home: eastern Africa
Order: Perching birds
Family: Starlings

 Grasslands

 Birds

© ERIC & DAVID HOSKING / CORBIS

A little smaller than the common starling, this bird is named for its "superb," jewel-like feathers. Perhaps the most beautiful starling in the world, the superb starling has a metallic-blue body and shiny-green wings. Both sexes are brilliant. Their young are a dull black until they are about a year old.

Like most birds in the starling family, this species is bold and fearless. It gathers in huge, noisy flocks in and around villages and towns in eastern Africa. The superb starling adds a splash of color to city parks. A starling flock spends most of the day on the ground, scratching through the dirt and sand.

After mating, a superb starling pair weaves a round, domed nest among the branches of a bush or between the large, sharp spines of a thorn tree. For building materials the couple uses a variety of grasses and sharp twigs. Some superb starlings move into a used nest, perhaps that of another bird or even a squirrel. The parents warm the eggs for 12 to 13 days, at which time the chicks hatch. Even after they learn to fly, the young starlings follow after their parents, begging for food.

Like their close relatives the mynahs and oxpeckers, starlings are intelligent birds. As evidence, they learn to adapt to civilization when humans move into the bird's natural habitats. Less adaptable species do not survive human changes nearly as well.

Blue Stentor
Stentor coeruleus

Length: about 1,000 micrometers
Diet: decaying plant and animal matter
Method of Reproduction: asexual
Number of Offspring: "parent" divides in two

Home: ponds worldwide, outside of permanently frozen polar regions
Order: Spirotricha
Family: Heterotricha

Fresh Water

Other Invertebrates

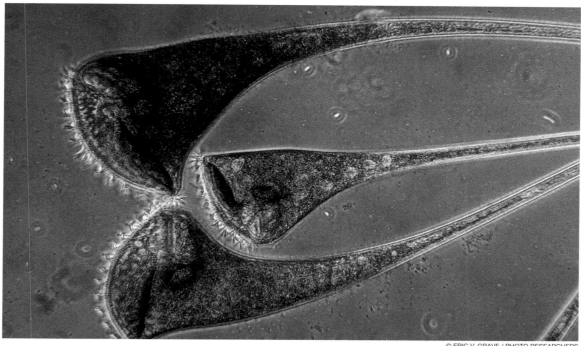

© ERIC V. GRAVE / PHOTO RESEARCHERS

If you were to look through a microscope at a drop of pond water, you would probably see many one-celled animals busily scooting about their microscopic world. One of the largest and prettiest is the blue stentor.

Stentors take their name form a mythical Greek hero. The Stentor of legend had a voice as loud as a trumpet. The tiny microbe stentor has a body shaped like a trumpet. The stentor's mouth is located at the wide end of its body. The smaller end is used to anchor the animal in place.

As you peer through your microscope, look carefully at the blue stentor's wide mouth. It is crowned with a wreath of tiny hairs called *cilia*. These cilia beat rhythmically, stirring up a microscopic whirlpool that draws tiny bits of food up and into the stentor's funnel-shaped mouth. If the blue stentor does not like what it tastes, it can reverse its cilia and sweep the particles back out of its mouth. By eating decaying plant and animal matter, pond microbes such as the blue stentor help purify our water.

Inside the stentor's one-celled body are special chemical-filled sacs, called *vacuoles*, that act like stomachs to digest food. A stentor excretes its waste through a hole in its body envelope called an "anal pore." This microbe can also draw itself into a sealed ball by tightening a row of elastic threads running the length of its body.

23

Stonechat
Saxicola torquata

Length: about 5 inches
Weight: about ½ ounce
Number of Eggs: 4 to 6
Home: Europe, Africa, and Asia

Diet: mainly insects
Order: Perching birds
Family: Thrushes, warblers, and flycatchers

Cities, Towns, and Farms

Birds

© LANS VON HORSTEN / GALLO IMAGES / CORBIS

Stonechats are among the most widely distributed of the world's perching birds. They live throughout Europe and in large portions of Central Asia. In the winter, many migrate to mild coastal regions along the shores of Great Britain, western France, and the Mediterranean. Others fly as far south as Ethiopia in Africa or to the edge of the tropics in southeastern Asia.

The stonechat is recognized by its dark, handsome plumage. The male has a black head, a rusty breast, and a distinct white neck patch. The female is a drab version of her mate. Chats (there are many species) are named for their distinctive chattering, which resembles the sound of smacking lips. They usually sing from high perches or while "dancing" through the air in a bouncy song flight.

This very lively perching bird hunts insects in the air and on the ground. It generally avoids dense vegetation and prefers partly planted areas, where it can easily spot its prey. In spring the male stonechat sings for a mate while spreading and showing off his tail and wings. Once mated, the pair builds a nest hidden among plants on the ground. Both parents share the duty of warming their red-speckled, bluish-green eggs. Cuckoos often try to raid the stonechat's nest, replacing its eggs with their own. However, the brave little stonechat will vigorously attack any cuckoo in sight, tearing at the larger bird's head feathers.

White Stork
Ciconia ciconia

Length: about 40 inches
Weight: about 7½ pounds
Number of Eggs: 3 to 5
Home: *Summer:* Europe, Asia, and northern and central Africa

Winter: southern Africa
Diet: frogs, reptiles, insects, and mollusks
Order: Storks and their relatives
Family: Storks

 Cities, Towns, and Farms

 Birds

☐ Summer ■ Winter

© NATURFOTO HONAL / CORBIS

? Endangered Animals

In many parts of the world, the much-loved white stork is the subject of legend. In European fairy tales, white storks deliver babies. In Africa, where the stork migrates in winter, it is thought to bring much-needed rain. On both continents a white stork nesting on a house is said to be a sign of good luck. Thanks in part to folk legends, the white stork has always been somewhat protected. For centuries, it has lived around humans, roosting near farmlands and small villages. Unfortunately, such rural areas are being quickly replaced by crowded suburbs and cities. Water pollution and habitat destruction have also reduced the white stork's population. At least one subspecies, the Oriental white stork, is endangered.

Although they are strong fliers, white storks must make frequent rest stops. As a result, they cannot fly over large bodies of water. In spring, migrating white storks avoid the long flight over the Mediterranean Sea by returning north from Africa by way of Morocco or Turkey.

Upon their arrival in Europe, white storks build huge stick nests at the tops of trees, haystacks, buildings, and human-made stork platforms. Mated pairs often return to their old nests each spring, making only minor repairs. The parents share egg-warming duties. When one stork relieves the other, both clatter their bill loudly in greeting.

Sungazer
Cordylus giganteus

Length: 8 to 15 inches
Diet: termites, beetles, grasshoppers, and spiders
Number of Young: 1 or 2

Home: southern Africa
Order: Lizards and snakes
Family: Girdle-tailed lizards

 Grasslands

 Reptiles

© ALAN BLANK / BRUCE COLEMAN

The sungazer loves to sunbathe, soaking up the rays with its head pointing up to the sky. In the morning the sungazer leaves its burrow and climbs onto a rock or a termite mound. There it sits almost motionless, for an hour or more. The creature's broad, flat body provides a large surface for soaking up heat from the sun. Once its body has warmed up, the sungazer begins to hunt. It relies on its good eyesight to find grasshoppers, spiders, and other prey.

The sungazer's triangular head and powerful body are covered with large, spiny scales. The scales are especially large on its tail and completely encircle it. This is the basis of the sungazer's family name, "girdle-tailed lizards."

As you might imagine, the sungazer's tail is a fearsome weapon. When defending itself against a predator, this reptile vigorously swings its tail back and forth. The sungazer lashes out at all enemies, even large, poisonous snakes.

Sungazers live in colonies in underground burrows in the grasslands and dry, rocky areas of southern Africa. There they either dig their own burrows or live in burrows made by rodents. Usually each burrow is home to a single sungazer. A female sungazer gives birth in her burrow in late summer, usually to two young. The babies are only about 5 inches long at birth.

Powder-blue Surgeonfish
Acanthurus leucosternon

Length: up to 12 inches
Diet: mainly algae
Home: coastal waters of the Indian Ocean and adjacent seas

Method of Reproduction: egg layer
Order: Perchlike fishes
Family: Surgeonfishes

 Oceans and Shores

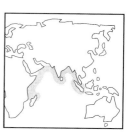

 Fish

© CARLOS ADOLFO SASTOGUE N. / SUPERSTOCK

"Looks can be deceiving" should be the powder-blue surgeonfish's motto. Although this bright, attractive fish seems harmless at first glance, it can actually be very dangerous. A pair of sharp spines, shaped like surgeon's knives, give the fish its name. Both sides of its body have a spine just in front of the tail; the surgeonfish can point the spines in different directions in order to attack predators—or people who carelessly handle it.

The powder-blue surgeonfish is oval, flat, and covered with small scales. It lives in and near coral reefs in warm tropical seas and eats both plant and animal matter. Most of its diet consists of algae, which it scrapes off rocks with its chisel-like teeth.

Surgeonfish mate in the early evening, as a pair swims to the surface. The female lays eggs, while the male releases sperm. The larvae that come out of the hatched eggs look so different from the adults that scientists once believed they were a different animal. After drifting awhile in the sea, the larvae sink to the bottom, where they develop the characteristics of the adults.

Because of its beautiful coloring, the powder-blue surgeonfish is popular in aquariums. However, it needs lots of room and large amounts of food. It's definitely not the kind of fish you could keep in a home aquarium.

Suricate (Meerkat)
Suricata suricatta

Length: 10 to 14 inches
Weight: 23 to 33 ounces
Diet: insects, small
   vertebrates, and birds' eggs

Number of Young: 2 to 5
Home: South Africa
Order: Carnivores
Family: Civets and mongooses

 Grasslands

 Mammals

© NIGEL J. DENNIS / GALLO IMAGES / CORBIS

This little meat-eater of the South African savanna is part of the mongoose family. Like the mongoose, the suricate has a long body and short legs. Its gray fur is striped with 8 to 10 crisscrossing black bands, and its eyes are outlined in black on a light-colored head.

The suricate's hind feet have powerful claws, which it uses to dig large tunnels in the ground. It uses these tunnels to live in, but it also finds underground prey in them. Suricates capture all sorts of insects, rodents, lizards, snakes, small birds, and eggs. Often they fight with each other over their prey.

During the day, suricates like to sun themselves next to the opening of their tunnels. At the least noise, they stand up like watchmen—as prairie dogs do—and they can stay propped up on their tails for a long time. Watching this way, suricates can warn the other members of the colony if their worst enemy, the bateleur eagle, comes near. Suricates live in groups of 10 to 15. They are very sociable and like to groom each other. They always leave their droppings in the same place.

Mating takes place from September through October, and the young are born between November and December. The female gives birth to 2 to 5 babies in a tunnel lined with grass. Nursed for 7 to 9 weeks, the young start to take their first solid food after the 6th week.

Common European Swallowtail
Papilio machaon

Wingspan: 3 to 4 inches
Diet: adult: plant nectar; larva:
  leaves of wild carrots
Method of Reproduction: egg
  layer

Home: Europe, Asia, and
  North Africa
Order: Butterflies and moths
Family: Swallowtails

 Grasslands

 Arthropods

© KIM TAYLOR / BRUCE COLEMAN INC.

The common European swallowtail is a large butterfly that can be recognized by the two tail-like projections on its back wings. These "tails" probably reminded people of the tails of swallows. Like other butterflies, the common European swallowtail has wings covered with tiny scales. Pigments in the scales give the wings their beautiful color.

The common European swallowtail is a strong flier. It comes to rest on a flower, takes a sip of nectar, then is off to visit another flower. It is a common sight during summertime in meadows, fields, forest clearings, and flowery roadside banks.

A European swallowtail passes through four stages in its life cycle: egg, caterpillar (larva), pupa, and adult. The caterpillar is striped in black and white, like a zebra, but with red dots breaking the black stripes. It has an unusual weapon called the osmeterium. This is a Y-shaped, orange-colored scent gland located in the caterpillar's back, just behind the head. Normally the osmeterium is inside the body. But when the caterpillar senses danger, it pushes the osmeterium out through a slit. The sudden appearance of the osmeterium scares off many birds and other predators. If a predator doesn't leave, the caterpillar gives off a foul-smelling gas from the osmeterium that is sure to send the predator fleeing for less-smelly prey.

Whooper Swan
Cygnus cygnus cygnus

Length: about 5 feet
Weight: about 20 pounds
Diet: leaves, stems, and roots
Number of Eggs: 3 to 5

Home: Europe and Asia
Order: Ducks and screamers
Family: Swans, geese, and ducks

 Fresh Water

 Birds

© MAURIZIO LANINI / CORBIS

Whoopers are the world's noisiest swans. Except when breeding, they gather in large flocks, bellowing an almost deafening, buglelike call. Migrating flocks usually fly high in the sky in a characteristic diagonal line or "V" formation. Their slow, powerful wingbeats make a soft, swishing noise.

Whooper swans feed day and night, either while wading through marshlands or floating across open water. As they graze, they paddle their feet, stirring up food from the bottom. Whoopers also dip their head into the water to search for underwater plants. In areas where marshlands have been destroyed, the swans graze in meadows and crop fields.

These swans generally mate for life, usually in their fourth or fifth year. In spring the couple breaks from the flock and establishes a nesting territory. There they build a mound of reeds and other plant matter some 2 feet high and 6 to 7 feet wide. The parents share nesting duties and later teach their chicks to find food. In fall the family rejoins the flock to fly south.

Whoopers are often confused with Europe's two other white swans: the mute swan and Bewick's swan. Bewick's is almost a foot shorter than the whooper. Mutes and whoopers can be distinguished by bill color; the mute's beak is orange, while the whooper's is bright yellow.

30

Swordtail
Xiphophorus helleri

Length: up to 6 inches
Diet: small organisms on the water's surface
Method of Reproduction: eggs that develop within the mother's body

Home: Central America; introduced elsewhere
Order: Topminnows and their relatives
Family: Live-bearing topminnows

 Fresh Water

 Fish

© BRUNO CAVIGNAUX / BIOS / PETER ARNOLD, INC.

Swordtails are well known to people who have home aquariums. In their native environment, swordtails are green fish with a yellow belly and a red zigzag line running along each side of the body. Swordtails raised for aquariums, however, come in many additional colors and patterns. There are red swordtails, black swordtails, white swordtails with pink eyes, and so on. People have produced these varieties by crossing, or breeding, swordtails that showed variation in color and pattern.

The swordtail gets its name from the lower part of the male's tail fin, which is long and pointed, just like a sword. A large male swordtail may be 6 inches long, with the tail making up about half this length. Females are usually smaller than males. During mating, the male sword tail fertilizes the eggs inside the female. The female does not lay the fertilized eggs. Instead, the eggs develop within her body, living on their own egg yolk.

In four to six weeks, the young fish have formed. Each fish breaks through the membrane of its eggs and leaves the mother's body. The young swordtails usually are born tailfirst. They are fully formed, but only about ½ inch long. They immediately begin to swim around in search of food. The male's "sword" develops when he is about one year old.

31

Himalayan Tahr
Hemitragus jemlahicus

Length: 4 feet (male); 3 feet (female)
Weight: 200 pounds (male); 80 pounds (female)
Diet: grasses and herbs
Number of Young: usually 1

Home: Himalaya Mountains of Asia; introduced elsewhere
Order: Even-toed hoofed mammals
Family: Bovines

 Forests and Mountains

 Mammals

© ZSSD / SUPERSTOCK

The high mountain habitat of the Himalayan tahr becomes very cold in winter. But the tahr has a built-in blanket! The animal is covered with a coat of long, shaggy hair, which provides a lot of insulation. On its neck and shoulders is a mane of soft hair. The adult buck (male) has a thick mane that may hang to his knees. The mane of the doe (female) and the young male is not as thick or as long.

Himalayan tahrs look very much like goats. Both males and females have short, flattened horns that curve backward. The horns are permanent; they are not shed. They are used for defense and for fighting among males at mating time. But the tahrs'

main defense is speed. They are gentle animals that would rather run away from leopards and other enemies than fight.

Himalayan tahrs are also social animals that live in groups called herds. The size of a herd varies from place to place, ranging from fewer than 20 animals to more than 75. Even larger herds have been seen in New Zealand, one of the places where these creatures have been successfully introduced.

Himalayan tahrs give birth to only one or two offspring a year. Baby tahrs are very well developed at birth and are able to stand and move with their mother when they are only a few hours old.

Scarlet Tanager
Piranga olivacea

Length: 6½ to 7½ inches
Wingspan: 11 to 12 inches
Diet: insects and other small invertebrates
Home: *Summer:* North America

Winter: Panama and South America
Number of Eggs: 3 to 5
Order: Perching birds
Family: Tanagers

 Forests and Mountains

 Birds

Summer
Winter

© ROGER TIDMAN / CORBIS

The scarlet tanager is one of the world's most beautiful birds. The male is particularly striking during the breeding season, when his feathers are a brilliant red and black. After breeding has ended, the male molts. He grows a new coat of feathers, with blackish wings and tail and a greenish-yellow head and body. The female is pale yellow, with dark markings on the wings and tail, colors that remain the same all year.

Every spring and fall, scarlet tanagers migrate a long distance. In spring, they fly to their breeding grounds in eastern North America. In fall, they fly south to Panama and northern South America.

The scarlet tanager is a tree dweller. It lives in forests, wooded parks, and large trees in people's yards. It feeds mainly on insects, which it finds in the treetops, in shrubs, and on the ground. In this way the scarlet tanager is very valuable to people because it eats many destructive pests, including aphids, gypsy-moth caterpillars, termites, and wood-boring beetles. The bird also feasts on worms, snails, and spiders, and adds berries and fruits to its diet in the fall.

The female builds a saucer-shaped nest on a secure limb of a large tree, often very high above the ground. There she incubates her eggs for about two weeks, until they hatch. Young tanagers are ready to leave the nest when they are about 11 days old.

Cat Tapeworm
Taenia taeniaformis

Diet: digested food from the host's intestine
Method of Reproduction: egg layer

Home: worldwide
Length: 6 to 24 inches
Order: Cyclophyllids
Family: Taeniids

 Cities, Towns, and Farms

 Other Invertebrates

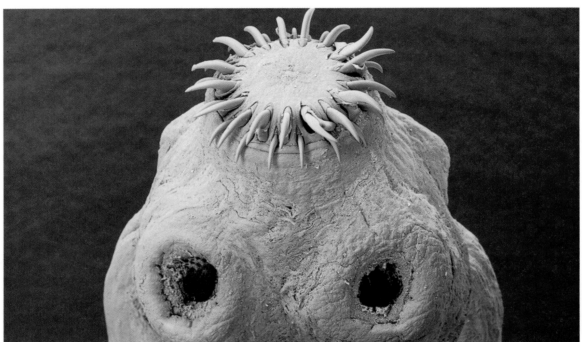

© OLIVER MECKES / PHOTO RESEARCHERS

The domestic cat has the unfortunate distinction of being the host to a number of different parasitic tapeworms. Among the most notorious of these parasites is one named the cat tapeworm. This long, flat worm inhabits the intestines of cats. If left unchecked, the tapeworm will eventually make the cat very ill and ultimately will kill it.

The adult worm attaches itself to the inner surfaces of a cat's intestines by means of a double row of hooks on the worm's head. The cat tapeworm does not need a mouth or a digestive system. It simply absorbs food through its body wall after the food has already been digested by the host cat.

This tapeworm is both male and female. The animal's body is constructed of many tiny square segments, each equipped with both sets of reproductive organs. When the segments farthest from the tapeworm's head are mature, they break free from the rest of the animal. They pass out of the cat's body in the cat's feces, or droppings.

When a mouse or rat eats food contaminated by the droppings, fertilized tapeworm eggs can enter their body. Inside a new host, the eggs hatch into larvae and pass from the rodent's digestive system into the bloodstream and the muscles. If a cat kills and eats a rodent, the larvae may enter the digestive system of the cat and develop into full-grown adult tapeworms.

Western Tarsier
Tarsius bancanus

Length of the Body: about 5 inches
Length of the Tail: about 9 inches
Diet: spiders, insects, small lizards, fish, and birds

Number of Young: 1
Home: Borneo and Malaysia
Weight: about 4 ounces
Order: Primates
Family: Tarsiers

 Rainforests

 Mammals

© FRANS LANTING / MINDEN PICTURES

The most noticeable characteristic of a tarsier is the size of its eyes compared with the rest of its head. If a person's eyes were as large in comparison, they would be the size of oranges. The tarsier's wide ears are also exaggerated. This nocturnal jungle creature has excellent eyesight and hearing. Tarsiers are named for their exceptionally long heel bones, or tarsi. The unique shape of the tarsier's feet and legs enable it to leap great distances.

Tarsiers were abundant in prehistoric times. Today there are only three living species, the largest of which is the western tarsier. Western tarsiers are quite quarrelsome. Each adult establishes a territory of up to 7 acres and fights viciously with intruding tarsiers. After a brief mating and a six-month pregnancy, the female gives birth to a single baby about half her size.

A hunting tarsier is fascinating to watch. As it perches on a tree branch or vine, it swivels its ears like independent radar antennae. Once the tarsier has pinpointed an interesting sound (such as a rustling bird), it rotates its head to face the direction of the sound. Using eyes and ears for orientation, the tarsier leaps through the air, lands on its prey, and bites it to death. The tarsier then jumps back to its perch to eat. Its ability to turn its head up to 180 degrees has long spooked the natives of Borneo, who consider the tarsier an omen of evil.

Lesser Hedgehog Tenrec
Echinops telfairi

Length: 5½ to 7 inches
Weight: about 3 ounces
Diet: insects and other
    invertebrates

Number of Young: 2 to 10
Home: Madagascar
Order: Insect eaters
Family: Tenrecs

 Forests and Mountains

 Mammals

© TOM MCHUGH / PHOTO RESEARCHERS

Of the 30 species of tenrec living on the island of Madagascar, two look amazingly like European hedgehogs. As its name implies, the lesser hedgehog tenrec is the smaller of the two. Like a true hedgehog, the hedgehog tenrec is thickly covered with long spines, which discourage predators from coming too close and biting. This species has one great advantage over European hedgehogs: it can climb trees. Despite its plump body, the lesser hedgehog tenrec is an agile acrobat that can scurry along slender branches and even leap from twig to twig.

The hedgehog tenrec is equally at home in the trees and on the ground. During the day, it sleeps under a log or rests in a tree hole. Lesser hedgehog tenrecs of the same sex often fight over a sleeping hole. But two of the opposite sex will gladly cuddle together for warmth. These tenrecs hibernate through the coldest months of winter.

Lesser hedgehog tenrecs mate in fall and sometimes in midwinter if a warm spell wakes them from sleep. The female hedgehog tenrec gets ready to give birth by busily cleaning the hollow in which she and her mate live. She lines her den with soft nesting material. Then, just before the babies are born, the mother forces the father out of their home. He will not be invited to return until the babies are old enough to leave.

Whiskered Tern
Chlidonias hybrida

Length: about 10 inches
Wingspan: about 30 inches
Diet: insects, small fish, and amphibians
Number of Eggs: usually 2 or 3

Weight: about 3 ounces
Home: Europe, Asia, Africa, and Australia
Order: Waders and gull-like birds
Family: Gulls and terns

 Fresh Water

 Birds

© DIETMAR NILL / FOTO NATURA / MINDEN PICTURES

The whiskered tern is the largest of the marsh terns, but it is much smaller than such oceangoing species as the common or arctic tern. As a group, terns are more slender and graceful than their close relatives the gulls. Their wings are long and narrow, and their bill is very slender and pointed. The whiskered tern has an especially sharp, dagger-shaped bill. The bird often mixes with other terns in large flocks and can be recognized by its slow, steady flight.

Whiskered terns hunt for insects, small fish, and frogs in freshwater ponds, marshes, and farm fields. Small groups often hunt together, flying abreast. When the tern spots something tasty, it hovers for a moment and then dives. Whiskered terns can snatch prey directly from the water or drop, feetfirst, in front of prey on dry land.

Whiskered terns live year round in flocks of 50 to 100 birds. In spring, couples mate and establish small personal territories within the larger colony. Each mated pair chases away other birds that come too close to their nest. The terns also stay alert for invading predators. The first tern to detect danger usually warns the others with a loud alarm call. By fall the new chicks are old enough to migrate with the flock. Whiskered terns fly thousands of miles to winter in the Middle East and the tropics of Africa and Southeast Asia.

Bleeding-heart Tetra
Hyphessobrycon rubrostigma

Length: up to 3 inches
Diet: mainly small insects and their larvae
Method of Reproduction: egg layer

Home: Colombia
Order: Carps and their relatives
Family: Characins

 Fresh Water

 Fish

© MARK SMITH / PHOTO RESEARCHERS

In popular usage a "bleeding heart" is someone who makes a great show of sympathy for a specific cause or person. But for a tiny fish called the bleeding-heart tetra, the term refers to the creature's bright red spots ("heart") found on each side of its body behind the head. These red spots stand in great contrast to the rest of the creature, which has a brownish-red upper half, a reddish-silver lower half, and an orange throat and belly.

With such beautiful coloration, it's no wonder that the bleeding-heart tetra is a popular fish in home aquariums. People with aquariums also appreciate this tetra's peaceful nature and its quick adaptation to an artificial environment.

If not for its popularity as an aquarium fish, few Americans would be aware of the bleeding-heart tetra. The fish is native to Colombia in South America, where it inhabits small bodies of fresh water, usually water overgrown with dense vegetation. In this protected habitat, the bleeding hearts live in groups, spending their days peacefully eating small insects and their larvae.

In its body structure, the bleeding heart is much like other fish. It is a narrow creature, flattened from side to side, with several small fins and two large fins. Like all fish, the bleeding heart depends upon its fins for swimming and steering.

Glowlight Tetra
Hemigrammus erythrozonus

Length: up to 1¾ inches
Diet: insects and other small invertebrates
Method of Reproduction: egg layer

Home: rivers in Guyana
Order: Carps and their relatives
Family: Characins

Fresh Water

Fish

© MARK SMITH / PHOTO RESEARCHERS

It's no secret when a female glowlight tetra is ready to breed: the fish's transparent skin allows you to see the eggs inside her body! When a male glowlight tetra catches sight of the eggs, he swims to the female, and the two "dance" around one another in the water. Then the female releases her eggs, the male releases his sperm, and the eggs are fertilized.

Glowlight tetras form groups called schools, or shoals, in the rivers of tropical jungles. Each of these attractive little fish has a red stripe running along both sides of its body. The stripe continues right onto the top halves of the eyes. This red stripe is so thin and straight that it looks like someone just painted it! Although male and female glowlight tetras look alike, the female is a little bit larger and plumper than the male.

Glowlight-tetra eggs hatch only 24 hours after fertilization. In their first few days of life, the young hang from water plants. The yolk from the egg's yolk sac provides each infant fish with food. When the tetra is only four days old, it begins to swim about and feed on tiny animals.

As an aquarium fish, the glowlight tetra is peaceful and lively. It can even reproduce in an aquarium if the conditions are right. Its home should contain clusters of fine-leafed plants in which the fish can spawn. But beware! As soon as the tetra has laid eggs, it should be moved to another aquarium. Otherwise, it might eat its own eggs!

Mistle Thrush
Turdus viscivorus

Length: 10 to 11 inches
Wingspan: 17 to 19 inches
Weight: about 4 ounces
Diet: insects, snails, worms, and fruits
Number of Eggs: 2 to 5

Home: Europe, Asia, and northern Africa
Order: Perching birds
Family: Thrushes, warblers, and flycatchers

 Forests and Mountains

 Birds

© JOHN HAWKINS / FRANK LANE PICTURE AGENCY / CORBIS

The mistle thrush is named for its fondness for mistletoe berries. It also enjoys eating cherries, strawberries, apples, and pears, as well as berries from yew and juniper bushes. Fruits and berries are its fall and winter food. In the summer, it prefers to catch large, juicy insects such as grasshoppers and beetle larvae.

A bold singer, the mistle thrush claims the highest treetops as song posts. This thrush sings in all types of weather, even on some of the windiest and rainiest days. And it flies as powerfully as it sings. After a flurry of strong wingbeats, the mistle thrush closes its wings and glides like an arrow.

Despite its bold song and flight, the mistle thrush is known as a shy bird. Until recently it avoided civilization, preferring to live in remote woods that were neither too thick nor too dry. The mistle thrush's favorite habitat is stands of tall trees surrounded by meadows and weeds. But recently some populations have overcome their fear of humans. In England and Ireland, for example, the bird has spread into gardens and orchards, as well as treed avenues and parks.

These thrushes can be distinguished by the large, dark spots on their belly. The bird's upper parts are a grayish-olive, with white fringes on the wings. Males and females look very similar.

Rock Thrush
Monticola saxatilis

Length: 7 to 7½ inches
Weight: 1½ to 2¼ ounces
Diet: insects and berries
Number of Eggs: 4 or 5

Home: Eurasia and Africa
Order: Perching birds
Family: Thrushes, warblers, and flycatchers

 Forests and Mountains

 Birds

Summer ☐ Winter ■

© O. ALAMANY & E. VICENS / CORBIS

The rock thrush is a shy bird that loves the cool, rocky mountainsides of Europe and Asia. It generally avoids cities and other active, populated areas. But in winter, when food is scarce, the rock thrush often moves into quiet gardens and vineyards. If you come upon the shy rock thrush in the wild, chances are it will quickly jump behind a boulder or dive down a steep, craggy cliff. The bird also broods its young among the rocks. Using twigs and rootlets, it builds a large, cup-shaped nest under a boulder or inside a crack in a rocky cliff.

In spring and summer, the rock thrush is a solitary bird. Except for its mate, the bird pays little attention to others of its kind. However, in fall and winter, rock thrushes gather in flocks. They travel to their warm "vacation" home in western Africa.

The rock thrush spends much of its time on the ground, hunting for insects. It also hunts insects from perches on trees, rooftops, and high wires. Like a miniature eagle, the thrush swoops down on large insects such as beetles and crickets. In summer the bird supplements its diet with berries.

The male rock thrush sings a beautiful, warbling song that carries far through the mountain valleys. As if inspired by his own music, he soars straight up in the air. The higher he goes, the louder and faster he sings. At the end of his song, the thrush silently glides back down to his perch.

41

Eurasian Common Toad
Bufo bufo

Length: 3 to 6 inches
Weight: up to 9 ounces
Diet: ants, earthworms, snails, spiders, flies, and bugs
Number of Eggs: 4,000 to 10,000

Home: Europe, northwestern Africa, and Asia to Japan
Order: Frogs, toads, and tree toads
Family: True toads

 Forests and Mountains

 Amphibians

© MICHAEL MACONACHIE / PAPILIO / CORBIS

The Eurasian common toad has few enemies . . . for good reason. If disturbed, it will squirt a milky, poisonous liquid from a gland behind its eyes. The toad can sting the eyes, nose, and mouth of any animal or human foolish enough to bite or handle it.

The Eurasian common toad's one enemy is the toad fly, *Lucilia*. This fly lays its eggs on the toad's back. When the larvae hatch, they crawl inside their host's nostrils and up into its brain. There the larvae feed on brain tissue. The unfortunate toad goes quite crazy and begins crawling about in broad daylight without any sense of where it is going. After a few days, the toad dies.

Despite this deadly parasite, Eurasian common toads remain quite abundant throughout Europe, Asia, and parts of Africa. This species' large population is especially obvious in May. During this month the toads hop through the forest by the thousands in search of a stream or lake. Like all toads the Eurasian common toad mates underwater.

Physicians once used the Eurasian common toad as a pregnancy test. Doctors would inject a woman's urine into a female toad. If the woman was pregnant, the toad would lay eggs within 24 hours. Certain chemicals, called hormones, in a pregnant woman's urine cause this reaction. Today faster and simpler methods have replaced the toad test.

Green Toad
Bufo viridis

Length: 2¼ to 3½ inches
Diet: insects, spiders, slugs, and other small invertebrates
Method of Reproduction: egg layer

Home: Europe, Asia, and northern Africa
Order: Frogs and toads
Family: True toads

Fresh Water

Amphibians

© DAVID A. NORTHCOTT / CORBIS

The green toad changes its color to blend with its surroundings. This helps to hide the toad from enemies—and from prey it hopes to catch. When the green toad sits in a sunny spot, it is light tan with bright-green spots sprinkled over its back and legs. But when it moves into a shady place, its whole body becomes a dark greenish brown. It takes about 10 minutes for the toad's color to change.

The green toad has excellent eyesight and an interesting way of catching its prey. When it sees an insect, it quietly follows the unsuspecting prey, flips out its long, sticky tongue, and, in a split second, draws the tongue and the insect back into its mouth.

In places with cold winters, the green toad spends the winter months hibernating in underground burrows. Then, during spring's first heavy rainfall, it leaves the burrow and finds a place to mate. The green toad mates in ponds, puddles, and other bodies of water. Males arrive at the breeding place first. To attract mates, the males sound a long, trilling whistle that can be heard from far away.

A female green toad produces from 7,000 to 12,000 tiny eggs. The eggs are laid in a string that may be as long as 13 feet! Very few eggs eventually develop into adult toads. Many of the eggs and tadpoles die or are eaten by predators.

Surinam Toad
Pipa pipa

Length: 4 to 7½ inches
Diet: mainly insects, insect larvae, and other small invertebrates
Number of Eggs: 40 or more

Home: northern South America
Order: Frogs and toads
Family: Tongueless toads

  Fresh Water

Amphibians

© JANE BURTON / BRUCE COLEMAN INC.

Surinam toads have very unusual mating and egg-laying behavior. The male holds the female, and they swim in vertical circles. At the top of the circle, the female releases a few eggs. These fall on the male's belly. At the bottom of the circle, the eggs fall onto the female's back. The male Surinam toad immediately fertilizes the eggs, which stick to the female's back. The circle "dance" is repeated a dozen times or more until all the eggs are fertilized.

In the days following mating, the skin on the female Surinam toad's back swells up. The eggs sink into the skin, each in its own little pocket. A lid forms over each pocket, enclosing the egg. About 10 weeks later,

young toads begin to pop out of the pockets. They look exactly like their mother, but they are less than 1 inch long.

The Surinam toad spends its life in water. The toes on its back legs are very long and connected with webs. These help the toad swim quickly through the water.

The creature spends much time sitting on the bottom of a pond with its long fingers spread out near its mouth. Each finger has a four-pointed, star-shaped tip and is very sensitive. Around the toad's mouth are flaps that wiggle in the water currents. When a small animal comes close to investigate these wiggling "worms," it touches the fingers. The toad lunges forward and grabs the victim with its wide mouth.

Set Index

A

adder **1**:5
adder, rhombic night **1**:6
African bat-eared fox **3**:42
African scorpion, giant **8**:16
African snail, giant **8**:37
African twig snake **8**:38
African wild dog **3**:20
agile frog **3**:44
agouti, orange-rumped **1**:7
Alaskan pika (collared pika) **7**:23
Algerian hedgehog **5**:11
alligator lizard, southern **5**:41
alpaca **1**:8
alpine newt **6**:43
American black vulture **10**:24
American crow **3**:8
American tree sparrow **9**:11
amphibians
　caecilian, Ceylonese **2**:10
　frog, agile **3**:44
　frog, burrowing tree **4**:5
　frog, common gray tree **4**:6
　frog, European tree **4**:7
　frog, gold **4**:8
　frog, marbled reed **4**:9
　frog, marsupial **4**:10
　frog, moor **4**:11
　frog, northern chorus **4**:12
　frog, ornate horned **4**:13
　frog, paradox **4**:14
　frog, pickerel **4**:15
　frog, pig **4**:16
　frog, red-legged **4**:17
　frog, strawberry poison dart **4**:18
　newt, alpine **6**:43
　newt, crested (warty) **6**:44
　salamander, common dusky **8**:13
　salamander, fire **8**:14
　spadefoot, European **9**:10
　toad, Eurasian common **9**:42
　toad, green **9**:43
　toad, Surinam **9**:44
anemone, opelet **1**:9
anemone, silver-spotted (gem anemone) **1**:10
angel shark, European **8**:22
anoa **1**:11
ant, leaf-cutter **1**:12
anteater, dwarf **1**:13
anteater, scaly (giant pangolin) **1**:14
arctic fulmar **4**:19
arctic hare **5**:7
argus, blue-spotted **1**:15
arrau (giant South American river turtle) **10**:14
arthropods **6**:18
　ant, leaf-cutter **1**:12
　backswimmer, common **1**:16
　beetle, cellar **1**:28
　beetle, checkered (bee-wolf) **1**:29
　beetle, European rhinoceros **1**:30
　beetle, forest dung **1**:31
　beetle, whirligig **1**:32
　butterfly, brimstone **2**:7
　butterfly, sail (scarce swallowtail) **2**:8
　cockroach, wood **2**:32
　cricket, bush (bush katydid) **2**:44
　cricket, European mole **3**:5
　cricket, Mormon **3**:6
　daphnia (water flea) **3**:37
　darner, blue-green **3**:12
　darner, green **3**:13
　fly, large bee **3**:40
　grasshopper, blue-winged wasteland **4**:36
　grasshopper, green valley **4**:37
　hawkmoth, broad-bordered bee **5**:10

horntail, large **5**:17
horsefly, cattle **5**:19
katydid, steppe **5**:26
locust, migratory **6**:5
louse, human-body **6**:7
mosquito, eastern malaria **6**:34
moth, common magpie **6**:35
moth, six-spot burnet **6**:36
prawn, common European (palaemon) **7**:33
scorpion, giant African **8**:16
sexton (burying beetle) **8**:20
snakefly **9**:5
spider, goldenrod **9**:14
swallowtail, common European **9**:29
tortoiseshell **10**:7
treehopper **10**:9
treehopper, oak **10**:10
white, marbled **10**:36
Atlantic cod **2**:33
Australian lungfish **6**:8
Australian sea lion **8**:17
axis deer (chital) **3**:14
azure-winged magpie **6**:13

B

backswimmer, common **1**:16
Baikal seal **8**:18
Baird's beaked whale **10**:34
bandicoot, large, short-nosed **1**:17
barb, half-banded **1**:18
barbet, crimson-breasted **1**:19
barnacle, common goose **1**:20
barracuda, Pacific **1**:21
basilisk, double-crested **1**:22
bat, Gambian epaulet **1**:23
bat, Honduran white **1**:24
bat, large mouse-eared **1**:25
bat-eared fox, African **3**:42
beaked whale, Baird's **10**:34
bear, sloth **1**:26
bearded vulture **10**:25
beaver, Eurasian **1**:27
bee fly, large **3**:40
bee hawkmoth, broad-bordered **5**:10
beetle, burying (sexton) **8**:20
beetle, cellar **1**:28
beetle, checkered (bee-wolf) **1**:29
beetle, European rhinoceros **1**:30
beetle, forest dung **1**:31
beetle, whirligig **1**:32
bee-wolf (checkered beetle) **1**:29
bird of paradise, greater **1**:33
birds
　barbet, crimson-breasted **1**:19
　bird of paradise, greater **1**:33
　bittern, Eurasian **1**:35
　bluebird, blue-backed fairy **1**:37
　booby, blue-footed **1**:38
　booby, brown **1**:39
　bower-bird, satin **1**:40
　bunting, corn **2**:5
　chickadee, black-capped **2**:23
　chicken, greater prairie **2**:24
　courser, cream-colored **2**:43
　crossbill, red **3**:7
　crow, American **3**:8
　crow, carrion **3**:9
　crow, fish **3**:10
　dove, laughing **3**:24
　duck, torrent **3**:26
　dunlin **3**:27
　eagle, tawny **3**:30
　finch, snow **3**:36
　flicker, red-shafted **3**:38
　flycatcher, fork-tailed **3**:41
　fulmar, arctic **4**:19
　goose, magpie **4**:33
　greenfinch **4**:38
　greenshank **4**:39
　grouse, double-banded sand **4**:40
　gull, great black-backed **5**:5

heron, little blue **5**:12
heron, nankeen night **5**:13
heron, purple **5**:14
hornbill, red-billed **5**:16
jacamar, rufous-tailed **5**:21
jacana, wattled **5**:22
lapwing **5**:31
lorikeet, musk **6**:6
macaw, blue-and-yellow **6**:11
macaw, military **6**:12
magpie, azure-winged **6**:13
manakin, red-capped **6**:15
martin, sand **6**:17
merganser, red-breasted **6**:19
nuthatch, Eurasian **7**:5
owl, great gray **7**:8
owl, scops **7**:9
owl, short-eared **7**:10
owl, tawny **7**:11
parakeet, rose-ringed **7**:13
parrot, king **7**:14
penguin, Galápagos **7**:16
penguin, gentoo **7**:17
petrel, southern giant **7**:19
pheasant, Reeve's **7**:20
pipit, water **7**:24
plover, spur-winged **7**:26
pochard, red-crested **7**:27
puffin, tufted **7**:35
quail, little button **7**:40
quetzal **7**:41
roller, common **8**:9
roller, lilac-breasted **8**:10
sandpiper, wood **8**:15
shag, imperial **8**:21
shelduck, common **8**:26
siskin, Eurasian **8**:30
sparrow, American tree **9**:11
sparrow, hedge **9**:12
sparrow, Java **9**:13
starling, superb **9**:22
stonechat **9**:24
stork, white **9**:25
swan, whooper **9**:30
tanager, scarlet **9**:33
tern, whiskered **9**:37
thrush, mistle **9**:40
thrush, rock **9**:41
toucan, keel-billed **10**:8
vireo, white-eyed **10**:21
vulture, American black **10**:24
vulture, bearded **10**:25
vulture, king **10**:26
vulture, lappet-faced **10**:27
wagtail, white **10**:28
wagtail, yellow **10**:29
waxbill, red-cheeked (cordon-bleu) **10**:30
waxwing, cedar **10**:31
weaver, grenadier (red bishop) **10**:32
whydah, pin-tailed **10**:37
wren, superb blue **10**:43
bishop, red (grenadier weaver) **10**:32
bitterling **1**:34
bittern, Eurasian **1**:35
black-backed gull, great **5**:5
black-backed jackal **5**:23
blackbuck **1**:36
black-capped chickadee **2**:23
black mamba **6**:14
black ruby **8**:11
black vulture, American **10**:24
bleeding-heart tetra **9**:38
blind cavefish **2**:20
blue-and-yellow macaw **6**:11
blue-backed fairy bluebird **1**:37
bluebird, blue-backed fairy **1**:37
blue-footed booby **1**:38
blue-green darner **3**:12
blue heron, little **5**:12
blue-spotted argus **1**:15
blue stentor **9**:23
blue-tailed day gecko **4**:24
blue-winged wasteland grasshopper **4**:36

blue wren, superb **10**:43
booby, blue-footed **1**:38
booby, brown **1**:39
bower-bird, satin **1**:40
bowfin **1**:41
bream, common **1**:42
brimstone butterfly **2**:7
broad-bordered bee hawkmoth **5**:10
brocket, red **1**:43
bronze catfish **2**:16
brown booby **1**:39
brush-tailed possum **7**:31
buffalo, water **1**:44
bunting, corn **2**:5
burnet moth, six-spot **6**:36
burrowing tree frog **4**:5
burying beetle (sexton) **8**:20
bushbuck **2**:6
bush cricket (bush katydid) **2**:44
butterfly, brimstone **2**:7
butterfly, sail (scarce swallowtail) **2**:8
butterflyfish, freshwater **2**:9
button quail, little **7**:40

C

caecilian, Ceylonese **2**:10
California legless lizard **5**:33
Cape girdled lizard, common **5**:34
Cape hyrax **5**:20
Cape monitor **6**:26
caribou (reindeer) **8**:7
carp, common **2**:11
carpet python **7**:36
carpet shell, crosscut **8**:27
carrion crow **3**:9
cat, European wild **2**:12
cat, Geoffroy's **2**:13
cat, Iriomote **2**:14
cat, ring-tailed **2**:15
catfish, bronze **2**:16
catfish, Congo **2**:17
catfish, glass **2**:18
catfish, shovelnose **2**:19
cat tapeworm **9**:34
cattle horsefly **5**:19
cavefish, blind **2**:20
cedar waxwing **10**:31
cellar beetle **1**:28
Ceylonese caecilian **2**:10
chamois **2**:21
checkered beetle (bee-wolf) **1**:29
chevrotain, water **2**:22
chickadee, black-capped **2**:23
chicken, greater prairie **2**:24
Chinese water deer **3**:15
chital (axis deer) **3**:14
chorus frog, northern **4**:12
chub **2**:25
chuckwalla **2**:26
cichlid, firemouth **2**:27
cichlid, lionhead **2**:28
civet, masked palm **2**:29
coati, ring-tailed **2**:30
cobra, king **2**:31
cockroach, wood **2**:32
cod, Atlantic **2**:33
coelacanth **2**:34
collared pika (Alaskan pika) **7**:23
colpeo fox **3**:43
column sponge, purple **9**:16
common backswimmer **1**:16
common bream **1**:42
common Cape girdled lizard **5**:34
common carp **2**:11
common dusky salamander **8**:13
common European prawn (palaemon) **7**:33
common European swallowtail **9**:29
common goose barnacle **1**:20
common goral **4**:34
common gray tree frog **4**:6
common gudgeon **4**:42

common langur **5**:30
common liver fluke **3**:39
common magpie moth **6**:35
common piddock **7**:21
common porpoise **7**:30
common roller **8**:9
common shelduck **8**:26
common shrew, Eurasian **8**:29
common toad, Eurasian **9**:42
common tree shrew **8**:28
conch, rooster-tail **2**:35
conger eel **3**:32
Congo catfish **2**:17
coolie loach **5**:43
coral, Devonshire cup **2**:36
coral, large star **2**:37
coral, northern stony **2**:38
coral, red precious **2**:39
coral, staghorn **2**:40
coral, star **2**:41
cordon-bleu (red-cheeked)
    waxbill **10**:30
corn bunting **2**:5
corn snake **8**:39
cottontail, New England **2**:42
courser, cream-colored **2**:43
crab-eating macaque **6**:9
cream-colored courser **2**:43
crested (warty) newt **6**:44
cricket, bush (bush katydid) **2**:44
cricket, European mole **3**:5
cricket, Mormon **3**:6
crimson-breasted barbet **1**:19
crossbill, red **3**:7
crosscut carpet shell **8**:27
crow, American **3**:8
crow, carrion **3**:9
crow, fish **3**:10
cup coral, Devonshire **2**:36

D

daboia (Russell's viper) **10**:20
dace **3**:11
daphnia (water flea) **3**:37
dark-green racer **7**:43
darner, blue-green **3**:12
darner, green **3**:13
deer, axis (chital) **3**:14
deer, Chinese water **3**:15
deer, fallow **3**:16
deer, pampas **3**:17
deer, red **3**:18
desert monitor **6**:27
Devonshire cup coral **2**:36
dhaman **3**:19
dog, African wild **3**:20
dogfish, spiny **3**:21
dollar, eccentric sand **3**:22
dolphin, Pacific white-sided **3**:23
dorcas gazelle **4**:23
Dory, European John **5**:25
double-banded sand grouse **4**:40
double-crested basilisk **1**:22
dove, laughing **3**:24
duck, torrent **3**:26
dung beetle, forest **1**:31
dunlin **3**:27
dusky salamander, common **8**:13
duster, magnificent feather **3**:28
duster, slime feather **3**:29
dwarf anteater **1**:13
dwarf mongoose **6**:24

E

eagle, tawny **3**:30
eastern malaria mosquito **6**:34
eccentric sand dollar **3**:22
echidna, long-nosed **3**:31
eel, conger **3**:32
Egyptian spiny mouse **6**:38
elephant, forest **3**:33
endangered animals
    anoa **1**:11
    cat, Iriomote **2**:14
    chamois **2**:21
    deer, pampas **3**:17
    dog, African wild **3**:20
    elephant, forest **3**:33
    gavial **4**:21
    gazelle, gazelle **4**:23

goat, wild **4**:32
guemal, Peruvian **4**:44
hog, pygmy **5**:15
horse, Przewalski's **5**:18
langur, common **5**:30
lemur, gentle gray **5**:32
moloch (silvery gibbon) **4**:28
monitor, desert **6**:27
monkey, Goeldi's **6**:30
monkey, woolly spider
    (muriqui) **6**:32
penguin, Galápagos **7**:16
pronghorn **7**:34
quetzal **7**:41
solenodon, Haitian **9**:8
stork, white **9**:25
turtle, giant South American
    river (arrau) **10**:14
epaulet bat, Gambian **1**:23
Eurasian beaver **1**:27
Eurasian bittern **1**:35
Eurasian common shrew **8**:29
Eurasian common toad **9**:42
Eurasian minnow **6**:21
Eurasian nuthatch **7**:5
Eurasian siskin **8**:30
European mink **6**:20
European mole **6**:22
European mole cricket **3**:5
European mouflon **6**:37
European perch **7**:18
European prawn, common
    (palaemon) **7**:33
European rhinoceros beetle **1**:30
European sole **9**:7
European spadefoot **9**:10
European swallowtail, common
    9:29
European tree frog **4**:7
European water vole **10**:23
European wild cat **2**:12
European wild rabbit **7**:42

F

fairy bluebird, blue-backed **1**:37
fallow deer **3**:16
false gavial **4**:22
feather duster, magnificent **3**:28
feather duster, slime **3**:29
featherworm, peacock **3**:34
filefish, orange-spotted **3**:35
finch, snow **3**:36
firemouth cichlid **2**:27
fire salamander **8**:14
fire sponge **9**:15
fish
    argus, blue-spotted **1**:15
    barb, half-banded **1**:18
    barracuda, Pacific **1**:21
    bitterling **1**:34
    bowfin **1**:41
    bream, common **1**:42
    butterflyfish, freshwater **2**:9
    carp, common **2**:11
    catfish, bronze **2**:16
    catfish, Congo **2**:17
    catfish, glass **2**:18
    catfish, shovelnose **2**:19
    cavefish, blind **2**:20
    chub **2**:25
    cichlid, firemouth **2**:27
    cichlid, lionhead **2**:28
    cod, Atlantic **2**:33
    coelacanth **2**:34
    dace **3**:11
    dogfish, spiny **3**:21
    eel, conger **3**:32
    filefish, orange-spotted **3**:35
    gourami, striped **4**:35
    gudgeon, common **4**:42
    John Dory, European **5**:25
    loach, coolie **5**:43
    loach, stone **5**:44
    lungfish, Australian **6**:8
    minnow, Eurasian **6**:21
    perch, European **7**:18
    piranha, white **7**:25
    reedfish **8**:6
    roach **8**:8
    ruby, black **8**:11

rudd **8**:12
shark, European angel **8**:22
shark, great hammerhead **8**:23
shark, Port Jackson **8**:24
sharksucker **8**:25
smelt, sand **8**:36
snipefish, longspine **9**:6
sole, European **9**:7
spadefish **9**:9
surgeonfish, powder-blue
    surgeon **9**:27
swordtail **9**:31
tetra, bleeding-heart **9**:38
tetra. glowlight **9**:39
triggerfish, redtooth **10**:11
triggerfish, undulate **10**:12
turbot **10**:13
unicornfish **10**:17
wels **10**:33
fish crow **3**:10
fishing (tentacled) snake **8**:44
flea, water (daphnia) **3**:37
flicker, red-shafted **3**:38
fluke, common liver **3**:39
fly, large bee **3**:40
flycatcher, fork-tailed **3**:41
flying possum, pygmy **7**:32
forest dung beetle **1**:31
forest elephant **3**:33
forest pig, giant **7**:22
fork-tailed flycatcher **3**:41
fox, African bat-eared **3**:42
fox, colpeo **3**:43
freshwater butterflyfish **2**:9
frog, agile **3**:44
frog, burrowing tree **4**:5
frog, common gray tree **4**:6
frog, European tree **4**:7
frog, gold **4**:8
frog, marbled reed **4**:9
frog, marsupial **4**:10
frog, moor **4**:11
frog, northern chorus **4**:12
frog, ornate horned **4**:13
frog, paradox **4**:14
frog, pickerel **4**:15
frog, pig **4**:16
frog, red-legged **4**:17
frog, strawberry poison dart **4**:18
fulmar, arctic **4**:19
fur seal, South American **8**:19

G

Gaboon viper **10**:19
Galápagos penguin **7**:16
Gambian epaulet bat **1**:23
gaur **4**:20
gavial **4**:21
gavial, false **4**:22
gazelle, dorcas **4**:23
gecko, blue-tailed day **4**:24
gecko, gliding **4**:25
gecko, Madagascar **4**:26
gecko, northern leaf-tailed **4**:27
gem anemone **1**:10
gentle gray lemur **5**:32
gentoo penguin **7**:17
Geoffroy's cat **2**:13
giant African scorpion **8**:16
giant African snail **8**:37
giant forest pig **7**:22
giant pangolin (scaly anteater)
    1:14
giant petrel, southern **7**:19
giant South American river turtle
    (arrau) **10**:14
giant tube sponge **9**:16
gibbon, silvery (moloch) **4**:28
gibbon, white-cheeked **4**:29
Gila monster **6**:33
giraffe, reticulated **4**:30
girdled lizard, common Cape
    5:34
glass catfish **2**:18
glass lizard, slender **5**:39
glider, yellow-bellied **4**:31
gliding gecko **4**:25
glowlight tetra **9**:39
goat, wild **4**:32
Goeldi's monkey **6**:30

golden-mantled ground squirrel
    9:20
goldenrod spider **9**:14
gold frog **4**:8
goose, magpie **4**:33
goose barnacle, common **1**:20
gopher snake **8**:40
gopher tortoise **10**:5
goral, common **4**:34
Gould's monitor **6**:28
gourami, striped **4**:35
grasshopper, blue-winged
    wasteland **4**:36
grasshopper, green valley **4**:37
grass snake **8**:41
gray lemur, gentle **5**:32
gray tree frog, common **4**:6
great black-backed gull **5**:5
greater bird of paradise **1**:33
greater kudu **5**:28
greater prairie chicken **2**:24
great gray owl **7**:8
great hammerhead shark **8**:22
green darner **3**:13
greenfinch **4**:38
greenshank **4**:39
green toad **9**:43
green tree python **7**:37
green valley grasshopper **4**:37
grenadier weaver (red bishop)
    10:32
grivet (savanna monkey) **6**:31
ground squirrel, golden-mantled
    9:20
grouse, double-banded sand **4**:40
guanaco **4**:41
gudgeon, common **4**:42
guemal, Peruvian **4**:44
guenon, moustached **4**:43
gull, great black-backed **5**:5

H

Haitian solenodon **9**:8
half-banded barb **1**:18
hammerhead shark, great **8**:23
hardun **5**:6
hare, arctic **5**:7
hartebeest **5**:8
hartebeest, hunter's (hirola) **5**:9
hawkmoth, broad-bordered bee
    5:10
hedgehog, Algerian **5**:11
hedgehog tenrec, lesser **9**:36
hedge sparrow **9**:12
helmeted lizard, smooth-headed
    5:40
helmeted turtle **10**:15
heron, little blue **5**:12
heron, purple **5**:14
Himalayan tahr **9**:32
hirola (hunter's hartebeest) **5**:9
Hoffmann's two-toed sloth **8**:33
hog, pygmy **5**:15
Honduran white bat **1**:24
hornbill, red-billed **5**:16
horned frog, ornate **4**:13
horntail, large **5**:17
horse, Przewalski's **5**:18
horsefly, cattle **5**:19
horsehair worm **10**:39
human-body louse **6**:7
hunter's hartebeest (hirola) **5**:9
hyrax, Cape **5**:20

I

ice cream cone worm **10**:40
imperial shag **8**:21
invertebrates, other
    anemone, opelet **1**:9
    anemone, silver-spotted (gem
        anemone) **1**:10
    barnacle, common goose **1**:20
    conch, rooster-tail **2**:35
    coral, Devonshire cup **2**:36
    coral, large star **2**:37
    coral, northern stony **2**:38
    coral, red precious **2**:39
    coral, staghorn **2**:40
    coral, star **2**:41
    dollar, eccentric sand **3**:22

duster, magnificent feather **3**:28
duster, slime feather **3**:29
featherworm, peacock **3**:34
fluke, common liver **3**:39
jellyfish, trumpet-stalked
(stauromedusan) **5**:24
mussel, swan **6**:40
nettle, sea **6**:42
orange, sea **7**:7
paw, kitten's **7**:15
piddock, common **7**:21
razor, pod **7**:44
shell, crosscut carpet **8**:27
slug, red **8**:35
snail, giant African **8**:37
sponge, fire **9**:15
sponge, purple column (giant
tube) **9**:16
sponge, stinker **9**:17
sponge, vase **9**:18
star, slime **9**:21
stentor, blue **9**:23
tapeworm, cat **9**:34
urchin, slate-pencil **10**:18
whelk, waved **10**:35
worm, horsehair **10**:39
worm, ice cream cone **10**:40
worm, peripatus velvet **10**:41
worm, red tube **10**:42
Iriomote cat **2**:14
Italian wall lizard **5**:35

J–K

jacamar, rufous-tailed **5**:21
jacana, wattled **5**:22
jackal, black-backed **5**:23
Japanese macaque **6**:10
Java sparrow **9**:13
jellyfish, trumpet-stalked
(stauromedusan) **5**:24
John Dory, European **5**:25
katydid, bush (bush cricket) **2**:44
katydid, steppe **5**:26
keel-billed toucan **10**:8
king cobra **2**:31
king parrot **7**:14
kingsnake, prairie **5**:27
king vulture **10**:26
kitten's paw **7**:15
kudu, greater **5**:28
kudu, lesser **5**:29

L

langur, common **5**:30
lappet-faced vulture **10**:27
lapwing **5**:31
large, short-nosed bandicoot **1**:17
large bee fly **3**:40
large horntail **5**:17
large mouse-eared bat **1**:25
large star coral **2**:37
laughing dove **3**:24
leaf-cutter ant **1**:12
leaf-tailed gecko, northern **4**:27
legless lizard, California **5**:33
lemur, gentle gray **5**:32
lesser hedgehog tenrec **9**:36
lesser kudu **5**:29
lilac-breasted roller **8**:10
lionhead cichlid **2**:28
little blue heron **5**:12
little button quail **7**:40
liver fluke, common **3**:39
lizard, California legless **5**:33
lizard, common Cape girdled
5:34
lizard, Italian wall **5**:35
lizard, lyre-headed **5**:36
lizard, sand **5**:37
lizard, short-horned **5**:38
lizard, slender glass **5**:39
lizard, smooth-headed helmeted
5:40
lizard, southern alligator **5**:41
lizard, wall **5**:42
loach, coolie **5**:43
loach, stone **5**:44
locust, migratory **6**:5
long-nosed echidna **3**:31

longspine snipefish **9**:6
lorikeet, musk **6**:6
louse, human-body **6**:7
lungfish, Australian **6**:8
lyre-headed lizard **5**:36

M

macaque, crab-eating **6**:9
macaque, Japanese **6**:10
macaw, blue-and-yellow **6**:11
macaw, military **6**:12
Madagascar gecko **4**:26
magnificent feather duster **3**:28
magpie, azure-winged **6**:13
magpie goose **4**:33
magpie moth, common **6**:35
malaria mosquito, eastern **6**:34
mamba, black **6**:14
mammals
agouti, orange-rumped **1**:7
alpaca **1**:8
anoa **1**:11
anteater, dwarf **1**:13
anteater, scaly (giant pangolin)
1:14
bandicoot, large, short-nosed
1:17
bat, Gambian epaulet **1**:23
bat, Honduran white **1**:24
bat, large mouse-eared **1**:25
bear, sloth **1**:26
beaver, Eurasian **1**:27
blackbuck **1**:36
brocket, red **1**:43
buffalo, water **1**:44
bushbuck **2**:6
cat, European wild **2**:12
cat, Geoffroy's **2**:13
cat, Iriomote **2**:14
cat, ring-tailed **2**:15
chamois **2**:21
chevrotain, water **2**:22
civet, masked palm **2**:29
coati, ring-tailed **2**:30
cottontail, New England **2**:42
deer, axis (chital) **3**:14
deer, Chinese water **3**:15
deer, fallow **3**:16
deer, pampas **3**:17
deer, red **3**:18
dog, African wild **3**:20
dolphin, Pacific white-sided
3:23
echidna, long-nosed **3**:31
elephant, forest **3**:33
fox, African bat-eared **3**:42
fox, colpeo **3**:43
gaur **4**:20
gazelle, dorcas **4**:23
gibbon, silvery (moloch) **4**:28
gibbon, white-cheeked **4**:29
giraffe, reticulated **4**:30
glider, yellow-bellied **4**:31
goat, wild **4**:32
goral, common **4**:34
guanaco **4**:41
guemal, Peruvian **4**:44
guenon, moustached **4**:43
hare, arctic **5**:7
hartebeest **5**:8
hedgehog, Algerian **5**:11
hirola (hunter's hartebeest) **5**:9
hog, pygmy **5**:15
horse, Przewalski's **5**:18
hyrax, Cape **5**:20
jackal, black-backed **5**:23
kudu, greater **5**:28
kudu, lesser **5**:29
langur, common **5**:30
lemur, gentle gray **5**:32
macaque, crab-eating **6**:9
macaque, Japanese **6**:10
marmot, Olympic **6**:16
mink, European **6**:20
mole, European **6**:22
mongoose, mongoose **6**:24
mongoose, white-tailed **6**:25
monkey, Goeldi's **6**:30
monkey, savanna (grivet) **6**:31

monkey, woolly spider
(muriqui) **6**:32
mouflon, European **6**:37
mouse, Egyptian spiny **6**:38
mouse, wood **6**:39
narwhal **6**:41
olingo **7**:6
pademelon, red-legged **7**:12
pig, giant forest **7**:22
pika, collared (Alaskan pika)
7:23
polecat, striped (zorilla) **7**:28
porcupine, tree **7**:29
porpoise, common **7**:30
possum, brush-tailed **7**:31
possum, pygmy flying **7**:32
pronghorn **7**:34
rabbit, European wild **7**:42
reedbuck, mountain **8**:5
reindeer (caribou) **8**:7
seal, Baikal **8**:18
seal, South American fur **8**:19
sea lion, Australian **8**:17
shrew, common tree **8**:28
shrew, Eurasian common **8**:29
sloth, Hoffmann's two-toed
8:33
sloth, three-toed **8**:34
solenodon, Haitian **9**:8
springbok **9**:19
squirrel, golden-mantled
ground **9**:20
suricate (meerkat) **9**:28
tahr, Himalayan **9**:32
tarsier, western **9**:35
tenrec, lesser hedgehog **9**:36
viscacha, plains **10**:22
vole, European water **10**:23
whale, Baird's beaked **10**:34
wolf, maned **10**:38
zebu **10**:44
manakin, red-capped **6**:15
maned wolf **10**:38
marbled reed frog **4**:9
marbled white **10**:36
marmot, Olympic **6**:16
marsupial frog **4**:10
martin, sand **6**:17
masked palm civet **2**:29
Mediterranean tortoise, spur-
tailed **10**:6
meerkat (suricate) **9**:28
merganser, red-breasted **6**:19
migratory locust **6**:5
military macaw **6**:12
mink, European **6**:20
minnow, Eurasian **6**:21
mistle thrush **9**:40
mole, European **6**:22
mole cricket, European **3**:5
moloch (lizard) **6**:23
moloch (silvery gibbon) **4**:28
mongoose, dwarf **6**:24
mongoose, white-tailed **6**:25
monitor, Cape **6**:26
monitor, desert **6**:27
monitor, Gould's **6**:28
monitor, Nile **6**:29
monkey, Goeldi's **6**:30
monkey, savanna (grivet) **6**:31
monkey, woolly spider (muriqui)
6:32
moor frog **4**:11
Mormon cricket **3**:6
mosquito, eastern malaria **6**:34
moth, common magpie **6**:35
moth, six-spot burnet **6**:36
mouflon, European **6**:37
mountain reedbuck **8**:5
mouse, Egyptian spiny **6**:38
mouse, wood **6**:39
mouse-eared bat, large **1**:25
moustached guenon **4**:43
muriqui (woolly spider monkey)
6:32
musk lorikeet **6**:6
mussel, swan **6**:40

N

nankeen night heron **5**:13

narwhal **6**:41
New England cottontail **2**:42
newt, alpine **6**:43
newt, crested (warty) **6**:44
night heron, nankeen **5**:13
Nile monitor **6**:29
northern chorus frog **4**:12
northern leaf-tailed gecko **4**:27
northern stony coral **2**:38
nuthatch, Eurasian **7**:5

O

oak treehopper **10**:10
olingo **7**:6
Olympic marmot **6**:16
opelet anemone **1**:9
orange-rumped agouti **1**:7
orange-spotted filefish **3**:35
oriental beauty snake **8**:42
oriental water dragon **3**:25
ornate horned frog **4**:13
owl, great gray **7**:8
owl, scops **7**:9
owl, short-eared **7**:10
owl, tawny **7**:11

P

Pacific barracuda **1**:21
Pacific white-sided dolphin **3**:23
pademelon, red-legged **7**:12
palaemon (common European
prawn) **7**:33
palm civet, masked **2**:29
pampas deer **3**:17
pangolin, giant (scaly anteater)
1:14
paradox frog **4**:14
parakeet, rose-ringed **7**:13
parrot, king **7**:14
peacock featherworm **3**:34
penguin, Galápagos **7**:16
penguin, gentoo **7**:17
perch, European **7**:18
peripatus velvet worm **10**:41
Peruvian guemal **4**:44
petrel, southern giant **7**:19
pheasant, Reeve's **7**:20
pickerel frog **4**:15
piddock, common **7**:21
pig, giant forest **7**:22
pig frog **4**:16
pika, collared (Alaskan pika)
7:23
pin-tailed whydah **10**:37
pipe snake, red-tailed **8**:43
pipit, water **7**:24
piranha, white **7**:25
plains viscacha **10**:22
plover, spur-winged **7**:26
pochard, red-crested **7**:27
pod razor **7**:44
poison dart frog, strawberry **4**:18
polecat, striped (zorilla) **7**:28
porcupine, tree **7**:29
porpoise, common **7**:30
Port Jackson shark **8**:24
possum, brush-tailed **7**:31
possum, pygmy flying **7**:32
powder-blue surgeonfish **9**:27
prairie chicken, greater **2**:24
prawn, common European
(palaemon) **7**:33
precious coral, red **2**:39
pronghorn **7**:34
Przewalski's horse **5**:18
puffin, tufted **7**:35
purple column sponge **9**:16
purple heron **5**:14
pygmy flying possum **7**:32
pygmy hog **5**:15
python, carpet **7**:36
python, green tree **7**:37
python, reticulate **7**:38
python, rock **7**:39

Q–R

quail, little button **7**:40
quetzal **7**:41

rabbit, European wild **7**:42
racer, dark-green **7**:43
razor, pod **7**:44
red-billed hornbill **5**:16
red bishop (grenadier weaver) **10**:32
red-breasted merganser **6**:19
red brocket **1**:43
red-capped manakin **6**:15
red-cheeked (cordon-bleu) waxbill **10**:30
red-crested pochard **7**:27
red crossbill **3**:7
red deer **3**:18
red-legged frog **4**:17
red-legged pademelon **7**:12
red precious coral **2**:39
red-shafted flicker **3**:38
red slug **8**:35
red-tailed pipe snake **8**:43
redtooth triggerfish **10**:11
red tube worm **10**:42
reedbuck, mountain **8**:5
reedfish **8**:6
reed frog, marbled **4**:9
Reeve's pheasant **7**:20
reindeer (caribou) **8**:7
reptiles
  adder **1**:5
  adder, rhombic night **1**:6
  basilisk, double-crested **1**:22
  chuckwalla **2**:26
  cobra, king **2**:31
  dhaman **3**:19
  dragon, oriental water **3**:25
  gavial **4**:21
  gavial, false **4**:22
  gecko, blue-tailed day **4**:24
  gecko, gliding **4**:25
  gecko, Madagascar **4**:26
  gecko, northern leaf-tailed **4**:27
  hardun **5**:6
  kingsnake, prairie **5**:27
  lizard, California legless **5**:33
  lizard, common Cape girdled **5**:34
  lizard, Italian wall **5**:35
  lizard, lizard **5**:37
  lizard, lyre-headed **5**:36
  lizard, short-horned **5**:38
  lizard, slender glass **5**:39
  lizard, smooth-headed helmeted **5**:40
  lizard, southern alligator **5**:41
  lizard, wall **5**:42
  mamba, black **6**:14
  moloch (lizard) **6**:23
  monitor, Cape **6**:26
  monitor, desert **6**:27
  monitor, Gould's **6**:28
  monitor, Nile **6**:29
  monster, Gila **6**:33
  python, carpet **7**:36
  python, green tree **7**:37
  python, reticulate **7**:38
  python, rock **7**:39
  racer, dark-green **7**:43
  skink, sand **8**:31
  skink, stump-tailed **8**:32
  snake, African twig **8**:38
  snake, corn **8**:39
  snake, gopher **8**:40
  snake, grass **8**:41
  snake, oriental beauty **8**:42
  snake, red-tailed pipe **8**:43
  snake, tentacled (fishing) **8**:44
  sungazer **9**:26
  tortoise, gopher **10**:5
  tortoise, spur-tailed Mediterranean **10**:6
  turtle, giant South American river (arrau) **10**:14
  turtle, helmeted **10**:15
  turtle, spotted **10**:16
  viper, Gaboon **10**:19
  viper, Russell's (daboia) **10**:20
reticulated giraffe **4**:30
reticulate python **7**:38
rhinoceros beetle, European **1**:30

rhombic night adder **1**:6
ring-tailed cat **2**:15
ring-tailed coati **2**:30
river turtle, giant South American (arrau) **10**:14
roach **8**:8
rock python **7**:39
rock thrush **9**:41
roller, common **8**:9
roller, lilac-breasted **8**:10
rooster-tail conch **2**:35
rose-ringed parakeet **7**:13
ruby, black **8**:11
rudd **8**:12
rufous-tailed jacamar **5**:21
Russell's viper (daboia) **10**:20

S

sail butterfly (scarce swallowtail) **2**:8
salamander, common dusky **8**:13
salamander, fire **8**:14
sand dollar, eccentric **3**:22
sand grouse, double-banded **4**:40
sand lizard **5**:37
sand martin **6**:17
sandpiper, wood **8**:15
sand skink **8**:31
sand smelt **8**:36
satin bower-bird **1**:40
savanna monkey (grivet) **6**:31
scaly anteater (giant pangolin) **1**:14
scarce swallowtail (sail butterfly) **2**:8
scarlet tanager **9**:33
scops owl **7**:9
scorpion, giant African **8**:16
seal, Baikal **8**:18
seal, South American fur **8**:19
sea lion, Australian **8**:17
sea nettle **6**:42
sea orange **7**:7
sexton (burying beetle) **8**:20
shag, imperial **8**:21
shark, European angel **8**:22
shark, great hammerhead **8**:23
shark, Port Jackson **8**:24
sharksucker **8**:25
shelduck, common **8**:26
shell, crosscut carpet **8**:27
short-eared owl **7**:10
short-horned lizard **5**:38
short-nosed bandicoot, large **1**:17
shovelnose catfish **2**:19
shrew, common tree **8**:28
shrew, Eurasian common **8**:29
silver-spotted anemone (gem anemone) **1**:10
silvery gibbon (moloch) **4**:28
sink, sand **8**:31
siskin, Eurasian **8**:30
six-spot burnet moth **6**:36
skink, stump-tailed **8**:32
slate-pencil urchin **10**:18
slender glass lizard **5**:39
slime feather duster **3**:29
slime star **9**:21
sloth, Hoffmann's two-toed **8**:33
sloth, three-toed **8**:34
sloth bear **1**:26
slug, red **8**:35
smelt, sand **8**:36
smooth-headed helmeted lizard **5**:40
snail, giant African **8**:37
snake, African twig **8**:38
snake, corn **8**:39
snake, fishing (tentacled) **8**:44
snake, gopher **8**:40
snake, grass **8**:41
snake, oriental beauty **8**:42
snake, red-tailed pipe **8**:43
snakefly **9**:5
snipefish, longspine **9**:6
snow finch **3**:36
sole, European **9**:7
solenodon, Haitian **9**:8
South American fur seal **8**:19

South American river turtle, giant (arrau) **10**:14
southern alligator lizard **5**:41
southern giant petrel **7**:19
spadefish **9**:9
spadefoot, European **9**:10
sparrow, hedge **9**:12
sparrow, Java **9**:13
spider, goldenrod **9**:14
spider monkey, woolly (muriqui) **6**:32
spiny dogfish **3**:21
spiny mouse, Egyptian **6**:38
sponge, fire **9**:15
sponge, purple column (giant tube) **9**:16
sponge, stinker **9**:17
sponge, vase **9**:18
spotted turtle **10**:16
springbok **9**:19
spur-tailed Mediterranean tortoise **10**:6
spur-winged plover **7**:26
squirrel, golden-mantled ground **9**:20
staghorn coral **2**:40
star, slime **9**:21
star coral **2**:41
star coral, large **2**:37
starling, superb **9**:22
stauromedusan (trumpet-stalked jellyfish) **5**:24
stentor, blue **9**:23
steppe katydid **5**:26
stinker sponge **9**:17
stonechat **9**:24
stone loach **5**:44
stony coral, northern **2**:38
stork, white **9**:25
strawberry poison dart frog **4**:18
striped gourami **4**:35
striped polecat (zorilla) **7**:28
stump-tailed skink **8**:32
sungazer **9**:26
superb blue wren **10**:43
superb starling **9**:22
surgeonfish, powder-blue **9**:27
suricate (meerkat) **9**:28
Surinam toad **9**:44
swallowtail, common European **9**:29
swallowtail, scarce (sail butterfly) **2**:8
swan, whooper **9**:30
swan mussel **6**:40
swordtail **9**:31

T

tahr, Himalayan **9**:32
tanager, scarlet **9**:33
tapeworm, cat **9**:34
tarsier, western **9**:35
tawny eagle **3**:30
tawny owl **7**:11
tenrec, lesser hedgehog **9**:36
tentacled (fishing) snake **8**:44
tern, whiskered **9**:37
tetra, bleeding-heart **9**:38
tetra, glowlight **9**:39
three-toed sloth **8**:34
thrush, mistle **9**:40
thrush, rock **9**:41
toad, Eurasian common **9**:42
toad, green **9**:43
toad, Surinam **9**:44
torrent duck **3**:26
tortoise, gopher **10**:5
tortoise, spur-tailed Mediterranean **10**:6
tortoiseshell **10**:7
toucan, keel-billed **10**:8
tree frog, burrowing **4**:5
tree frog, common gray **4**:6
tree frog, European **4**:7
treehopper **10**:9
treehopper, oak **10**:10
tree porcupine **7**:29
tree shrew, common **8**:28
tree sparrow, American tree **9**:11

triggerfish, redtooth **10**:11
triggerfish, undulate **10**:12
trumpet-stalked jellyfish (stauromedusan) **5**:24
tube sponge, giant **9**:16
tube worm, red **10**:42
tufted puffin **7**:35
turbot **10**:13
turtle, giant South American river (arrau) **10**:14
turtle, helmeted **10**:15
turtle, spotted **10**:16
twig snake, African **8**:38
two-toed sloth, Hoffmann's **8**:33

U-V

undulate triggerfish **10**:12
unicornfish **10**:17
urchin, slate-pencil **10**:18
vase sponge **9**:18
velvet worm, peripatus **10**:41
viper, Gaboon **10**:19
viper, Russell's (daboia) **10**:20
vireo, white-eyed **10**:21
viscacha, plains **10**:22
vole, European water **10**:23
vulture, American black **10**:24
vulture, bearded **10**:25
vulture, king **10**:26
vulture, lappet-faced **10**:27

W

wagtail, white **10**:28
wagtail, yellow **10**:29
wall lizard **5**:42
wall lizard, Italian **5**:35
warty (crested) newt **6**:44
wasteland grasshopper, blue-winged **4**:36
water buffalo **1**:44
water chevrotain **2**:22
water dragon, oriental **3**:25
water flea (daphnia) **3**:37
water measurer **6**:18
water pipit **7**:24
water vole, European **10**:23
wattled jacana **5**:22
waved whelk **10**:35
waxbill, red-cheeked (cordon-bleu) **10**:30
waxwing, cedar **10**:31
weaver, grenadier (red bishop) **10**:32
wels **10**:33
western tarsier **9**:35
whale, Baird's beaked **10**:34
whelk, waved **10**:35
whirligig beetle **1**:32
whiskered tern **9**:37
white, marbled **10**:36
white bat, Honduran **1**:24
white-cheeked gibbon **4**:29
white-eyed vireo **10**:21
white piranha **7**:25
white-sided dolphin, Pacific **3**:23
white stork **9**:25
white-tailed mongoose **6**:25
white wagtail **10**:28
whooper swan **9**:30
whydah, pin-tailed **10**:37
wild cat, European **2**:12
wild dog, African **3**:20
wild goat **4**:32
wolf, maned **10**:38
wood cockroach **2**:32
wood mouse **6**:39
wood sandpiper **8**:15
woolly spider monkey (muriqui) **6**:32
worm, horsehair **10**:39
worm, ice cream cone **10**:40
worm, peripatus velvet **10**:41
worm, red tube **10**:42

X-Y-Z

yellow-bellied glider **4**:31
yellow wagtail **10**:29
zebu **10**:44
zorilla (striped polecat) **7**:28